DAYDREAMS & NIGHTMAREZ

Mary'ah "Mo'zArt" Onwukwe

Daydreams & Nightmarez
Copyright © 2022 by Mary'ah "Mo'zArt" Onwukwe

All rights reserved. No part of this book may be reproduced or transmitted in any form or by any means without written permission from the author.

ISBN: 979-8-9873559-0-9

DEDICATION

First and foremost, I want to give honor to my Lord and Savior. I am so grateful that He saved me. I also want to thank Him for blessing me with so many creative gifts that I can share to others. I can't thank Him enough; He has brought through so much and I am truly grateful. It's why I write about Him so much. I feel like He speaks to me through poetry. I also feel like at times He speaks through me and some of my poems didn't feel like my own words but His. I love the Lord beyond what words can!

Next, I would like to dedicate a portion of this book to one of my closest friends and mentors in poetry, Demarco "Marco" Polk. When I sent him a draft of me just venting about my feelings, he told me that I had written poetry and urged me to perform the poem at his open mic night. With some gentle pushing, I got on stage and performed, Just Once (a poem in the book). So many people enjoyed my piece and told me about how I did so well for my first performance and that they could relate a lot to my poem. A few days later, he called me to tell me about how people were raving about my piece and wanted me to perform again. I had only written that poem, so to perform again meant that I had to write more poems, and ever since then, I've been writing poetry. Poetry is now one of my many loves that I didn't even think I could write so it's only right that he's a part of my dedication. He has been there every step of the way to helping me find my rhythm and flow in writing poetry to helping me perform my poems better. He always loves to hear new work I've created and never gets annoyed by it. He's also been such an encouraging friend to help me overcome doubts and insecurities when it came to sharing my art. He's a really great friend when I need one, so, I want to thank him for being himself.

Following him, I would like to dedicate this book to my grandfather, Bishop William E. Gaines Jr. He is such a wonderful pastor and teacher of the Gospel that I am always left wanting for more of his knowledge and wisdom. Quite a few poems are inspired by his sermons because they touched my spirit so, and I felt like I had to share it with others. He inspires me to help people every day through his dedication to God and the ministry. I love him so very much and I'm so thankful to have been blessed to have him in my life.

Last but certainly never least, I'd like to dedicate a portion of this book to my wonderful mother, Maria Gaines-Onwukwe. She has helped me with so much in life and has become like a best friend to me. She is my superwoman and inspires me daily. She is always there if I have a problem or just need a pep talk to keep from going crazy. She's the best mom a daughter could ask for and then some. I love her soooo much and she will forever have a special place in my heart.

INTRODUCTION

This book is a sky in motion. It holds both the light and the dark, not as opposites, but as companions. The sun and the moon do not compete. They take turns. They yield to one another. They teach us that life is lived in phases, not permanent states. *Daydreams & Nightmarez* follows that rhythm. We begin in the dark.

New Moon. There is a kind of emptiness that has weight to it. The kind that arrives after betrayal, after loss, after the moment you realize something in your life has shifted and will never return to what it was. The new moon is not dramatic. It is quiet. It is the hollow feeling in your chest when the world keeps moving but you feel paused inside it. These poems live in that stillness, in the first ache, in the beginning of nights that feel longer than they should.

Sunrise. Even the longest night cannot stop the morning. Sunrise is gentle. It does not rush you. It simply arrives, slowly pushing back the dark. These poems live in the early moments of healing, when life is just starting to feel lighter, when hope feels fragile but real, when the clouds begin to thin and you realize you are still here.

First Quarter. Healing is not quiet for long. The first quarter is the struggle to keep moving while carrying what hurts. It is smiling when you are tired. It is pretending everything is fine because explaining the truth feels heavier than silence. These poems speak of loneliness, of wanting someone to ask if you are okay and meaning it, and of fighting battles no one else can see.

High Noon. This heat of the day arrives. High noon is energy. It is momentum. It is the season of ambition and motion, when you begin chasing dreams again, when you start reclaiming pieces of yourself that you thought were gone. These poems carry laughter, drive, and the determination to build something meaningful with your life.

Full Moon. Pain has a way of returning when the world grows quiet. The full moon is intense. It is the night when emotions feel too loud to ignore, when the weight of everything presses against your ribs and breathing feels like hard labor. These poems speak of drowning feelings, of exhaustion, and of fighting to stay when leaving sometimes feels easier.

Golden Hour. These are moments when the light feels softer and kinder. Golden hour is for recognition. It is learning your worth without needing permission. It is confidence that grows slowly and quietly, until one day you realize you are standing differently, speaking differently, and eventually living differently. These poems are about purpose, about self-respect and becoming at home within yourself.

Last Quarter. These are the darkest moments that are overwhelmingly raw, loud, and honest. The last quarter is where the pain is no longer softened or hidden. It is the part of the journey where everything spills out, where you stop pretending to be strong and simply tell the truth about how much it hurts. These poems do not look away from the dark. They sit in it, speak it, and let it be seen.

Sunset. These are moments built in peace, after surviving for so long. This peace is not the kind that answers every question or guarantees tomorrow will be easy, but the quiet understanding that whatever comes, you will endure it. Sunset is for acceptance. It is the calm at the end of the day and the reminder that every ending makes room for another beginning. If the day was heavy, it is over now. If it was beautiful, there will still be more beauty ahead. These poems rest in that peace, in the soft certainty that life keeps moving, and so will you.

    The sun and the moon move in cycles. So do we. Some days you will feel like sunrise. Some nights you will feel like the last quarter of the moon. Sometimes both will exist in the same heart, at the same time. This book is not a straight path, on purpose. It is a sky, and every phase you meet here is a part of becoming the best version of yourself.

TABLE OF CONTENTS

New Moon 13
- When A Daddy's Girl Grows Up Without A Father 14
- Just Once 19
- Chemically Imbalanced 22
- Last Time 27
- Thief In The Night 29

Sunrise 37
- Weightless 39
- I Cannot But I Can 41
- Rejection Is God's Redirection 46
- Every Time I Say Goodbye 49
- Don't Cry Me A River 53

First Quarter 55
- Smile 56
- Painter's Touch 59
- Contradiction 62
- You Had One Job 64
- Failing Grades 66

High Noon 73
- Completed Work 74
- I Made It 78
- The Perfect Answer 80
- Separate To Elevate 83
- Shine, Star, Shine 86

Full Moon 93
- Is It Me? 94
- Why Am I So Different? 96
- Is That All I'm Worth? 101
- Ugly Duckling 106

Pick Me 109
Golden Hour 115
    Your Choice 116
    Shameful To Shameless 119
    Diamond In The Mud 123
    Who Am I? 126
    Hidden Treasure 128
Last Quarter 135
    Monsters 136
    Shattered 138
    Twisted Strings 143
    Residue 147
    Fallen Soldier 150
Sunset 155
    Power Couple 156
    The Eye Of The Storm 159
    God's Hand 162
    Healing Wounds 169
    Poetry Saved Me 174
About The Author 183
About Mo'zArt Creationz 184

NEW MOON

DAYDREAMS & NIGHTMAREZ

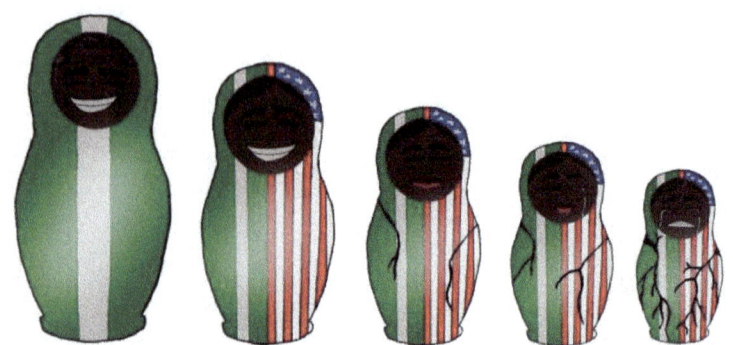

WHEN A DADDY'S GIRL GROWS UP WITHOUT A FATHER

What happens when a daddy's girl grows up without a father?
In short, a lot.

It's worse when you grow up without a father,
not because he died, but because he was absent.
It plants the seeds of doubt and abandonment,
and they are watered by the thoughts of me feeling far less than
adequate for him to have considered staying.
It sprouts into me thinking that if I'm not good enough
for my own father, I'll never be good enough
for anyone, including myself.

I remember the day he left, it still brings tears to my eyes,
knowing that that day, I couldn't cry,
not because I didn't want to
but because the tears that overflowed
from my mother and younger brother's eyes
had dried up the wells of mine.

MARY'AH "MO'ZART" ONWUKWE

Even at 10 years old,
I knew that in their weakness,
they needed someone who was strong,
even if it was a front.
My heart splintered into a million pieces at the sight.
Turning my gaze upon my baby brother who was two
at the time, devouring his dinner in peace without a clue
about what was happening around him.
I knew I needed to be strong for him too.
The splintered pieces of my heart decomposed
leaving a void to take its place.

On that day, I learned to compartmentalize my pains
and bury them to the deepest parts of my mind.
What isn't in the forefront, I can't see.
What I refuse to think about, can't hurt me.
That should make things better, right?
Wrong!
Because what I shielded myself from seeing
and refused to think about, manifested itself in other ways.
A young girl who was once nurtured by her father's love,
is now in search of it.
I know you have all heard the saying,
looking for love in the wrong places,
well, that was me, looking for a love I'll never find.

The last day I saw you in person was behind a glass window,
something an eleven-year-old shouldn't have experienced.

DAYDREAMS & NIGHTMAREZ

I blame you for the trauma I have now.
You could have fought to stay in this country.
You could have fought to be with your family.
But you were too much of a coward.
You let yourself be deported to Nigeria.

I had to spend holidays with a salty taste in my mouth
knowing that my family was now incomplete
while you used our broken pieces to build
a new family for you to take care of.
Why couldn't we be enough for you?
Why couldn't I be enough for you?

You robbed my childhood from me
because I ended up becoming a second mother to your seed
while my mother slaved to provide for us.
My younger brother got to spend time outside with his friends
while I babysat. Can you guess who missed school
because their baby brother was sick?
It was your babygirl who couldn't allow herself
to be a baby anymore.
Now in her adulthood, she can't help but to act like a baby
at times. She collects stuffed animals every chance she gets,
she throws tantrums instead of voicing why she's hurt
and she loves watching animated movies and cartoons.
She wants to stop but it's the only way she feels safe
because it reminds her of a time when you were still here.

MARY'AH "MO'ZART" ONWUKWE

Many years down the road, the phone calls that were consistent,
fizzled out. Eventually when you did call, it was never to ask
how I was doing, but always to speak to my younger brother.
My heart cracked and chipped apart each time
because all I wanted was for you to fill that void again
that you caused
but you just made it deeper.
This could explain why I hardly shared my feelings
and voiced my concerns because they were always disregarded
by the first man in my life. It only repeated with every man
I let in after him like a broken record.

I missed out on you teaching me lessons about love,
forcing me to seek outside education.
Education that came with a price.
It cost me my dignity, my self-worth, and my body.
Desperate for love, I gave away valuable parts of me
at a young age to undeserving men
because that seemed like the only way to get it.

Instead of you teaching me how to be treated like royalty,
I learned, from the guys around me,
how to accept breadcrumbs and the bare minimum
because that's all they made me feel like I deserved.
Since you abandoned me, it has become the norm.
You broke more than my heart when you left.
And now I have to try and repair what I didn't break.

DAYDREAMS & NIGHTMAREZ

I went from being a daddy's girl
to a girl with daddy issues.
Hard to love because I find it hard to trust.
Insecurities on top of insecurities.
Love will never find me
because you left me.

What happens when a daddy's girl grows up without a father?
A lot.

MARY'AH "MO'ZART" ONWUKWE

JUST ONCE

Just once, I want a guy to say he wants me
and shows it consistently.
Just once, I want to feel wanted.
Just once, I want to go on a date,
a real date, not no "Netflix and chill",
like you planned a whole night for us
cuz you wanna see me smile.
Just once, I want to be loved, valued, and respected by a man.
Just once, I want a man to show me off proudly.
Just. Once.

Just once, I want to be seen for my brains and personality,
not just a piece of meat, a sneaky link, or a booty call.
Just once, I want a guy to be honest with me,
no matter how hurtful it is, instead of ghosting
or causing arguments for no reason,
especially when I'm not what he wants.

DAYDREAMS & NIGHTMAREZ

Just once, I don't want to be cheated on, used, or abused.
Just once, I want to be chosen.
Just once, I want to feel a love
that doesn't require a heartbreak first.
Just once, I want to experience true happiness,
nothing temporary, but one that's long-lasting.
Just. Once.

Just once, I want to love myself fully
from the roots of my scalp
to the soles of my feet and not stop
because one guy doesn't see my worth.
Just once, I want to meet a guy that checks off
all the things on my checklist.
Just once, I'd like to meet a guy who wants to strengthen
his relationship with God, and actually show it with his actions.
Just once, I don't want to meet a guy who is still living
that street life, cuz let's be honest,
do I come across as a nigga's trap queen?
Just once, I'd love to meet a guy who is educated and ambitious.
Just. Once.
Maybe twice.

Just once, I want to be catered to and taken care of by a guy,
without ulterior motives.
Just once, I want to experience a love so free, and so beautiful,
that I don't lose sight of my passions.
Just once, I want to meet a guy who's supportive

MARY'AH "MO'ZART" ONWUKWE

of me and my dreams like if I wanted to reach for the sky,
he'll say "Nah, baby, reach for the stars."
Just once, I want to experience a life
where I'm not triggered by past traumas.
Just once, I'd love to experience
ALL these things.
Just.
Once.

DAYDREAMS & NIGHTMAREZ

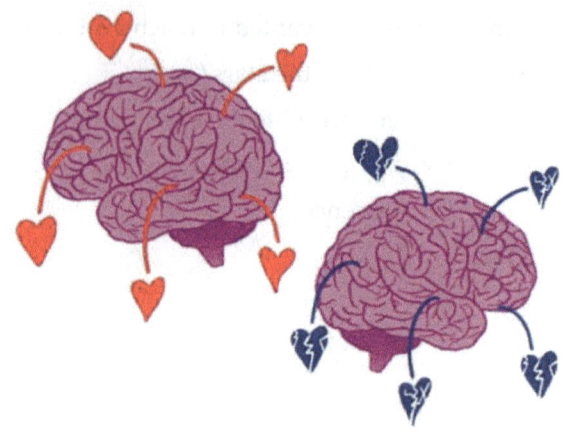

CHEMICALLY IMBALANCED

When I first laid eyes upon you,
it wasn't love at first sight,
but addiction.
It all started with a crush.
Seeing your brown eyes complementing your melanated skin
sent dopamine and serotonin to flood my brain.
Why am I so happy whenever you are near?
What is this blissful feeling that I can't shake
when I see your smile?
I feel like I'm floating on cloud nine
whenever my mind reminisces on the sweet nothings
you whispered in my ear that I can't stop daydreaming about.
"Is this what love feels like?"
I often wondered as my younger self.
"No, my sweet child."
Is what I would now answer.

MARY'AH "MO'ZART" ONWUKWE

"Not even close."
Because then obsession starts.
Why can't I stop thinking about you?
Why do I wait by the phone wishing
that the next notification is from you?
Why do I want to be around you all the time?
It's not enough that we can cuddle and be boo'd up.
I want to live in your skin and be always with you
because you make me so happy.

And then my brain releases adrenaline and norepinephrine.
Why am I suddenly so nervous around you?
Why does my heart skip a beat when you say my name?
Why do I squeal in my head
when your body would brush up against mine?
It doesn't stop there
because now all judgment and logic go out the window.
My brain shuts off my amygdala and silences my frontal cortex,
so that I can't think clearly when I'm around you.
My mind goes blank whenever I want to initiate a conversation.
After a while, I realize that I don't need school,
my friends, or family, because all I need is you.
I don't question that you only text me at night
or when you need something.
I don't question that your reasoning was
that you are "busy at work", or "sleep",
even though you were active on social media all day.
Maybe oxytocin is to blame.

DAYDREAMS & NIGHTMAREZ

Your hugs, kisses, and false reassurances
are like superglue that keep me stuck on you.
You could do no wrong in my eyes
that are blinded by your love.
No one else could compare to you.
The pedestal that I put you on was so high,
that I couldn't even reach it.
Maybe that's why you looked down on me.
Maybe that's why you left me.
It's now that I realized that your love was a drug,
and now I'm an addict.

Ya know, fighting an addiction is hard,
especially when you feel like you have no help.
It's better to stick to my lonesome
than to be reminded that no one understands
how much I am hurting from craving your love,
time, and attention,
and not being able to receive it.

They tell me to "Get over it."
Don't you think I've tried?!
I can't help that my brain is starving for the dopamine
that came from seeing your beautiful face
and spending quality time with you.
I can't help that it's starving for the serotonin
that made me feel like the happiest

MARY'AH "MO'ZART" ONWUKWE

and luckiest woman alive
to have been blessed with a guy like you.
I can't even help that it's starving for the oxytocin
that made me long for your touch.
I really miss your kisses,
they always left me wanting for more.

You see, I've been gluttonously feeding my brain these things
for months to years building a higher tolerance each time.
So, no, I can't just
"Get. Over. It!"

All he left me was access to view his social media.
And even that was too much
because every chance I could,
I checked it to examine if there had been any changes.
Did he follow someone new?
He *did*.
Is she pretty?
She *is*.
As I scan over her profile,
I can see the multitude of likes and comments from him.
He must really like her. I bet he likes her better than me.
My eyes burn and my vision blurs
when I realize that I'm not wanted.

Each day that my brain starves,
it makes me suffer along with it.

DAYDREAMS & NIGHTMAREZ

I can't sleep because in my dreams
all I see is you, and it's too painful to bear.
I've lost all motivation to do my schoolwork,
let alone live.
The nights pass me by and it's harder to recall what day it is.
Is it Monday?
Wednesday?
Ugh, who cares,
because it's just another day without your love.

To stop the constant suffering,
I tried to recreate the feeling
that your love gave me
with temporary flings.
But I could never make the right concoction
because something was always missing.
You.

Maybe this is my punishment for wanting your love.
You've intoxicated me beyond repair.
I just wish that you'd have given me the antidote to your poison
before leaving me chemically imbalanced.

MARY'AH "MO'ZART" ONWUKWE

LAST TIME

Who knew the last time would be the last time?
Now I'm stuck thinking 'bout you during every pastime.
Thinking about the way you held me so close,
and told me you loved me,
where I could see the smile on your face that I caused,
where you talked about the future between you and me,
and it wasn't just romantically.
It was one where our passions collided in perfect harmony.
Where I can share my art and you can share ya thoughts.
Where we can be ourselves, thriving off of happiness
that not even money could've bought.
I'd give the world just to have one more moment with you.
You were like my best friend.
My confidant.
We separated
and now I am lost.

DAYDREAMS & NIGHTMAREZ

No one knows about the sleepless nights
wishing you could hold me again.
No one knows about how my ears ache
to hear you speak my name once more.
and to hear your laugh
that always made me giggle along with you.
No one knows about the bucket of tears I've collected
to one day wash the memory of you from my brain.
Because it'd be easier to forget
than to remember
that the last time was the last time.

MARY'AH "MO'ZART" ONWUKWE

THIEF IN THE NIGHT

All throughout my childhood,
I had been told about how Jesus would come back
like a thief in the night to take his people.
Yet, no one ever told me what to do after
falling in love with a mere man who felt dignified
to take what didn't belong to him in the darkest hours.
I didn't knowingly fall in love with him.
Originally, I had fallen in love with someone
who I thought would be my forever person.
But I later learned it was his charming facade
that had me blind to his hidden intentions.
A beautiful lie. Before the theft,
I was a whole being with a whole identity and purpose.
You loved that I could strip my mind and heart of their essence
and put it into words so that others could think and feel like me.

DAYDREAMS & NIGHTMAREZ

You loved my personality and how I trusted others without end
and saw the good in everyone.
You loved how I could give you the clothes off my back
and my last dollar even if it meant
I had to be naked and broke.
You loved that you had a personal cheerleader
that rooted for you while my stands became barren.
If I was all these things to you,
how could you steal from me?
Why did you steal from me?

You came like a thief in a night when I least expected it.
It didn't all happen at once,
no, you were methodical and patient.
You swiped a piece at a time,
so that I wouldn't notice.

Month after month,
things started disappearing.
You stole the piece of my identity
that now makes me numb
to any other advances from men.
I thought I acted like this
because I loved you so much.
Now, I know, it's because I'd rather count
individual grains of sand at the beach
than go through this again.
You stole the piece of my identity

MARY'AH "MO'ZART" ONWUKWE

that made me overly kind and wanting to help others.
My mind twisted in knots
trying to figure out why I was more reserved and guarded.
Now, I know, it's because my heart barricaded itself
inside of tall brick walls,
so that it wouldn't be bruised and beaten again.
You stole the piece of my identity
that made me want to be creative.
No longer did the pen and paper call to me to make magic,
their voices had been kidnapped and taken as hostages.
You stole the piece of my identity
that made me strive for my dreams.
No longer did I aspire to have a white coat ceremony
or have my books sell out on bookshelves.
You stole the piece of my identity
that made me want to go to church and read my Bible.
I halted my relationship with God
because I felt that my relationship with you mattered more.
You stole the piece of my identity
that made me want to be around family and friends.
No one ever could understand
why I enjoyed your company more,
so, it was best to distance myself entirely.
They just had to be haters of us
and what we could be.
How wrong I had been for not believing them.
You stole the piece of my identity
that made me laugh and enjoy life.

DAYDREAMS & NIGHTMAREZ

You abandoned me which left me wanting
to abandon this earth.
Nothing was funny
about how you had stolen
all these pieces of my identity.

Where does this act of grand theft leave me?
I am now empty.
Just a void.
A space.
No more.
You've taken every part of me,
and now there's nothing left
Why did you steal from me?
Why did you steal from me?

You've left me here in this hollow shell,
clinging onto life.
No longer do I live,
I just exist.
I float around waiting to be sucked up by life's vacuum
so that I can stop grieving
the loss of my identity,
this loss of my being,
and your betrayal.
Why did you steal from me?
Why did you steal from me?

MARY'AH "MO'ZART" ONWUKWE

If it isn't bad enough,
I've had to watch you escape
with the prized parts of me
and I couldn't do anything about it.
This level of expertise required practice.
I couldn't have been the test run.
I am not the only woman you have done this to.
No, this could have only been executed, so perfectly,
after years of trial and error.
I was just a quick scheme in your grand heist
to expand your fortune.
Why did you steal from me?
Why did you steal from me?

With nowhere to go,
I floated to a place where I could find help.
It happened to be my home. My refuge. In there, I found God
and fell to my knees as I cried out,
"Lord, what do I do?
He came as a thief in the night and robbed me.
I have nowhere else to turn to. Please help me."

And He looked down at me and said, "Why…
do you give yourself away to people who cannot
give you what you desire?"

I sat there confused. "What do you mean?
I didn't give these pieces away. He stole them!"

DAYDREAMS & NIGHTMAREZ

And the Lord told me, "No,
when you decided that you wanted their love
more than Mine, you gave them away.
Because involving yourself in an earthly love
that isn't centered by the love for Me,
will just result in a love where one person takes
and the other gives
endlessly.

You didn't realize it
but you had loosened up those parts of yourself
for him to take it when you were not aware.
You gave him access to your prized possessions,
the prized parts of your personality, your being.
You trusted him more than you would listen to Me
and that is why you now have no identity.
But I love you, My Child,
and I know you did not do this on purpose.
You just had gotten so caught up in trying to search for a love
that cannot compare to Mine that you lost sight
in protecting your heart and protecting those parts of you.

But it is okay, My Child.
I will restore you and put you back together
better than before.
Those parts of you that he stole will be refined and upgraded
because you have an insurance policy
that My Son paid the price for.

MARY'AH "MO'ZART" ONWUKWE

So, no longer will you be just an empty void,
you will be an overflowing presence
that can be felt and seen from miles away.
Now that I have restored you,
it will take you time
to get used to your new body and interacting with others
because now, you'll be more cautious.

Just as the thief has escaped,
there will be many more
to come and take his place.
They'll have different names,
but underneath their masks,
they'll have the same face.
So beware,
the thief in the night."

SUNRISE

DAYDREAMS & NIGHTMAREZ

MARY'AH "MO'ZART" ONWUKWE

WEIGHTLESS

Feeling the water beneath my feet brings peace.
I dive deep into the ocean to release my problems.
But there's always one problem
that doesn't want to release me,
Depression,
the big Loch Ness Monster
that dwells in the trenches.

It wraps itself around me and squeezes me dry of confidence.
It nips at my self-worth
and makes me beg for permanent rest
because I feel I do not deserve to survive.
The blood of my sins haunts me
as it stains the surrounding water.
My chest tightens from the pressure
and my head feels as though it may detonate
at any moment.
A ticking time bomb
that only had seconds left.

As the air escapes me, and bubbles filled with my screams
rise to the surface and release my cries into the atmosphere,
my will to fight diminishes.
My eyes close in anticipation of my fate.

Little did I know that I was never alone,
that someone *had* heard my cry for help.

DAYDREAMS & NIGHTMAREZ

He loosens the grip of the beast
who was reluctant to let go,
but follows its master's commands.
My frail body starts to float
as I ascend to the surface.
He wraps His arms around me,
and His warmness surrounds the coldness
that encases my near-lifeless form.
He breathes onto me
and my eyes spring open
as my body breaks the surface.

A breath of fresh air. Totally rejuvenated.
Levitating in the atmosphere,
I can't see my Savior's face, but I can feel His presence.
The overwhelming love and peace I feel,
brings tears to cascade down my face like an avalanche.
Pure bliss.

I've waited so long for a feeling like this.
Forever floating as He lets me know
that I am never alone
because He will always be there for me.
He brings Heaven down to Earth.

No longer am I drowning under the weight
of the big Loch Ness Monster named Depression.
Because of My Savior, I am now weightless.

MARY'AH "MO'ZART" ONWUKWE

I CANNOT BUT I CAN

You cannot
Like a clot, those words are plastered across my heart
as I stand before an obstacle that will not depart
from in front of my dreams.
I tried pushing the obstacle out of the way
and I scream as it never once wavered.
I've tried walking around it, but it never enabled me
as it matched my steps to prevent me from reaching my purpose.
After a few bruises from my battle
and dirtied clothes from my falls, my solace
disappears as I realize…
I cannot.

The obstacle smiles as it crosses its arms, as a taunt
knowing that it has me beat.
My body runs away as I feel the weight of defeat
wash over me. The obstacle laughed behind me.

DAYDREAMS & NIGHTMAREZ

Who am I to think I could fulfill such a dream, seriously?
I am a nobody,
Nothing special to any degree.

A voice behind me spoke, "You *were* a nobody.
But not anymore."

Turning around, I saw Jesus, my mentor,
with a bright aura surrounding Him.
I told Him, "I don't understand what you mean. I am a wimp.
A nobody. I cannot even get around the obstacle in my way."

He says, "My Child, I love you so much that I suffered to pay
My Life so that I, being holy and clean,
could come into your unclean and corruptible body to intervene
against the wages of sin to save your soul.
And when I saved you and entered your heart,
you became whole.
You became somebody.
You became special to have in Me and My Father's company.
You can do all things through Me who can strengthen you."
He steps forward, touches my shoulder and on me, He blew.
Inhaling His breath, I received the Holy Spirit.

A surge of energy sprouts from where He touched,
without limit, to the rest of my body rejuvenating me.
"I feel power." I tell Jesus with glee.

MARY'AH "MO'ZART" ONWUKWE

He smiles and tells me, "Because of the Holy Spirit.
It's deliberate when it enables you to overcome your flesh
which is sinful, destructive, and will only cause you stress.
When the spirit says yes, your flesh says no.
When the spirit says you can,
the flesh will say that you can't although
the Holy Spirit empowers you to overcome the natural man
and make it submit to it. With the Holy Spirit's assistance,
I can work on you from the inside out
to blot out areas of resistance."

"I just don't understand.
I have trauma and I am dirty
from the times I've fallen into sin.
I give up too early.
I am so unworthy for you to work on.
There's no way I am strong enough to go above and beyond
to conquer this obstacle. It's possible
you chose the wrong person."

Jesus says, "I make no mistakes. I know who you are for certain.
I know who you are going to be.
I need you to understand that yes,
you *can* overcome any obstacle. Because I said you can.
You are blessed
so, you *will* triumph over the flesh.
You *can* make it obey."

DAYDREAMS & NIGHTMAREZ

"I-I just don't know how to make confidence stay."

He commands, "Repeat after me: I can. God told me I can.
And keep saying it until you believe."

I did as told and immediately started to receive.
Each new utterance of those words
caused that same power surge to return.
Stronger and Stronger.
My skin started to tingle and slightly burn.
My flesh fighting for power brought me to my knees.
Something wanted to burst out, so on my blouse, I squeezed.
Grabbing at the buttons, it opened with one thrust.
The struggle was over. My body took a second to adjust
to the power coursing through my bloodstream.
I looked down and my clothes changed. In the seams,
was a blue super-suit with a red and gold cross emblem.

Looking up at Jesus confused, I asked,
"Where did this suit stem from?"

He answers, "You needed to change
in order to fully embrace the power.
You needed to enter a secret place away from the enemy,
a strong tower
so that I could change you into something new
and help you to become superhuman.
You must pray more, fast more, read My Word more,

believe more in Me and explore your new identity.
There is enough power to do everything
I have called you to do with intensity
and be victorious.
Now go back to that obstacle,
put up your dukes and fight.
Be filled with My Light
and go pursue your destiny."

Standing tall, I went back to the obstacle
and it slightly expressed unease.
It covered its surprised expression
and became more determined to hinder my dreams.
With intentions to injure,
it stepped forward
and ordered, "You cannot."

I declared, "Yes, I can. I will remove you from that spot."
A series of punches and slams later,
the obstacle whimpered back to where it came from
and my back became straighter.
Grabbing the door to my future,
I realized that whatever obstacle comes my way,
that I can overcome it because God told me that I can today.

DAYDREAMS & NIGHTMAREZ

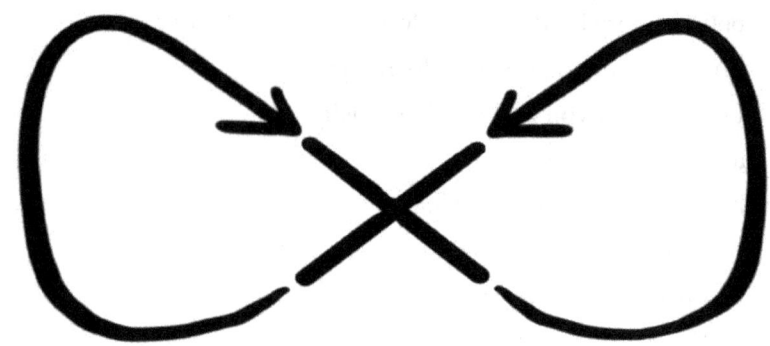

REJECTION IS GOD'S REDIRECTION

Sometimes your blessings are in the redirection.
So, rejection isn't really rejection,
but projection
to be who you were meant to be in the first place.
Because had God allowed you to be a part of the selection,
You would've become comfortable in the deflection
of your true purpose and missed the true connections
that God wanted you to make.

You see, through Jesus' resurrection,
we are made whole and powerful.
But we allow life to inject us with self-hatred and doubts
that cause a disconnection from God.
Now we suffer from an infection that causes us to wander about
searching for genuine love and affection that we won't find.
But God loved us enough to make an objection
by performing a thorough inspection of us
to find blots of darkness and cast it out.

MARY'AH "MO'ZART" ONWUKWE

As He makes the correction,
He touches our minds and hearts
and tells us that we hit roadblocks in our life
for our own protection because sometimes
He wants us to trust that He has everything under control.

He reminds us through the recollection
of all the times He has brought us through,
that He will not abandon us.
He wants us to also remember that He is perfection
and we are not, so, we should stop killing ourselves
trying to be perfect and just be our best.
And when you feel like the weight of the world
is on your shoulders, and you feel like you are all alone
with no help, just remember:
that rejection is just God's redirection
to your true destination.

DAYDREAMS & NIGHTMAREZ

MARY'AH "MO'ZART" ONWUKWE

EVERY TIME I SAY GOODBYE

There are seasons in my life that require time to heal my voids
and crazily enough it's the time I most heavily avoid
because to heal means to hurt
for a while. So, it makes perfect sense
as to why this phenomenon occurs.

Every time I say goodbye,
I revisit sweet memories that have turned sour
and leave a bitter taste in my mouth
because there was nothing that I could do to prevent the loss.
So, instead of facing my problems head on, I run from them.
I begin the dangerous thought that if I outrun them,
then they can't catch up to me and cause me to stumble.
But they always did come back to bite me in the–
assets that remind me of you
and won't get lost in the disarray of my grieving process.
Now the wound that I once had is now bigger,
and much deeper.
It's gotten so bad that I cannot keep running,
it hurts too much.
I must sit and take time to dress them, so they can finally heal
but that means I must finally address them
and acknowledge its presence.
I must admit to myself that these wounds that bleed are real
and not a figment of my imagination, that takes strength.
Strength that I don't always have as I confront these scary pains.

DAYDREAMS & NIGHTMAREZ

The human body can do powerful things when stressed,
especially as a means for survival.
It can repress the memories that are too hurtful to relive
to where they are locked under pad and key
and buried deep into the abyss of my mind.
But healing is a process that somehow finds
those buried keepsakes that have been locked
and thrown away into a sea of forgetfulness
and allows me to remember it.
It cuts through the lock
and shoves the problem into my face,
so that I can't ignore it.

Every time I say goodbye,
I realize that healing is never easy
because in order to heal, I must forgive,
forgive those who lied to me,
forgive those who left me,
and forgive the person who wronged me the most:
me.
A lot of the times I knew better,
but didn't choose to do better
and now I sulk in the company of regret.
I blame myself for not reaching certain goals
and being more ahead in life.
I blame me for putting myself into situations
that halted my progress and blocked my blessings.
The list could continue for centuries

MARY'AH "MO'ZART" ONWUKWE

but there's no use in dwelling in shoulda, woulda, coulda's
as forgiveness is a tricky concept.
They say forgiveness is not for the other person but for you.
It's a gift that you give to release the pain
that you have been harboring inside.
If that's the case, then why can't I open my mouth
to form those three words:
"I forgive you"?

After searching my brain for an answer, I find one:
I can't say goodbye.
To let go of the hurt I've endured,
I must let go of the person who caused it.
To say, "I forgive you",
means that I am ready to say goodbye,
but I am not.

I am learning that every time I say goodbye,
I allow myself to grieve as a part of the healing process.
I know that life moves on,
and that it doesn't stop for anyone
but I should stop for myself
to acknowledge the pain that I've been ignoring.
I can't keep holding in my pain
because I have too many things to do.
I need to remind myself that it is okay to cry
and mourn the loss I've experienced,
past or present.

DAYDREAMS & NIGHTMAREZ

Every time I say goodbye,
I realize that healing is such an up and down process
where I feel great one day, and horrible the next
and that is okay and a part of life.
I am learning that just because I allow myself to grieve
when I need to, that I cannot forget to live.
It may sound contradictory,
but grief and living life can coexist together
as roommates in the house of growth.
Grief, instead of overtaking my life
and cluttering my home with sadness,
will start to clean up after itself.
As I live my life, I can help Grief pick up the pieces,
so that they aren't so painful to remember.
Occasionally, I'll get reminders of my pain,
but they won't overtake my life again
because I've learned to live with it.

Now every time I say goodbye,
I smile instead of running.

MARY'AH "MO'ZART" ONWUKWE

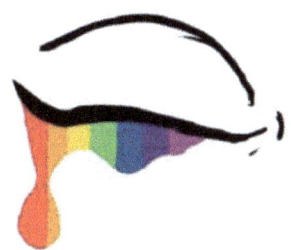

DON'T CRY ME A RIVER

Don't cry me a river, instead, cry me a rainbow.
Rivers are cold and destructive
and care nothing about whom it devours.
Its currents sweep you off your feet
until you are left to drown in the sea of your emotions.
Allowing the river to grow, only plants the seed of destruction.
Destruction of your happiness,
your mind,
and even your well-being.
So don't cry me a river, cry me a rainbow instead.

Rainbows are the beacon of peace and serenity after the storm
to let you know that it's over and that everything will be okay.
Its bold colors appearing in the sky are your reminder
that despite the hardships you may face
and how many times life has knocked you down,
that you will survive this and learn to get back up again.
You will overcome your situation.
It will pass and you will heal from it.

DAYDREAMS & NIGHTMAREZ

The rain that showers from your eyes
will water the ground you walk on
as you plant the seed of revival.
Revival of the person you always wanted to be.
Revival of the love for the hobbies that once made you smile.
Revival of your joy that will sprout again with time.
And when it does, please remember
not to allow the clouds of other people to block your rainbow
because your warm rays deserve to be felt by the world.

FIRST QUARTER

DAYDREAMS & NIGHTMAREZ

SMILE

Smile!
Smile for the camera please!
For the people are watching you through their lenses,
and you don't want them to capture how broken you are,
so, Smile!
Even if it's fake.
Smile!
Even though you'd rather be in a different place.
Smile!
Because they say it helps to keep from crying.
Smile!
Because it takes more energy to frown
so please don't mind my Smile!
Because I barely slept last night,
and I need to conserve my energy to make it through the day.
Smile!
My dimples impale my cheeks

MARY'AH "MO'ZART" ONWUKWE

because I smile so hard and can't stop.
My friends and family think I'm doing alright
because they never see me without a
Smile!
Everyone tells me I have a beautiful smile,
well, what good does that do me if I still feel ugly inside.
I'm breaking down and no one can see it because of my
Smile!
I've run out of I'm fine's and I'm good's.
My heart is bleeding and I'm choked up on my own blood,
so sorry if I can't speak right now,
all I can give you is
my Smile.
I don't want them to ask questions so therefore,
I have to keep my Smile.
Because who really wants to hear
about how I'm deteriorating inside?
No one's gonna help, so therefore,
I gotta get through this by myself and smile.
Why can't they see through this smile
and realize that I'm not happy?
Maybe it's my fault,
I'm too good of an actor putting on too good of a show.
Because if they could, they'd see through it, right?
They should be able to see through my tired eyes
and know that something is off, right?
Or are they too blinded by my smile,
that convinces them that maybe I am okay.

DAYDREAMS & NIGHTMAREZ

I wonder how many people smile
even when they don't wanna.
I wonder how many people smile
and give me the same fake smile that I give them
because they're broken inside too,
but they can't afford to let it show.
I smile
because life continues to move on
whether I am moving or not.
My smile
may brighten up your day
while it just reminds me of
how dark mine is.
When will this pain end?

Smile...
because it's the only thing I can do.
Smile...
because I'm praying for better days.
Smile...
because this feeling can't last forever,
so, why won't it leave?
Smile...
because one day,
this smile,
won't be fake, so, until then,
I have to keep faking
my smile.

MARY'AH "MO'ZART" ONWUKWE

PAINTER'S TOUCH

As soon as you smiled and said, "Hello",
I had my easel, canvas, and brush ready.
You began to tell me about yourself
and I dipped my brush in water then in paint.
Applying my brush to the canvas, I stroked away,
sketching out all the possibilities of what we could be.

Stepping back to examine the sketch,
I determined that you'd be perfect for me.
The more time we spent together,
the more detailed my painting became.

DAYDREAMS & NIGHTMAREZ

Over time, I fell in love more with the portrait I painted
than the subject standing right in front of me
because you had imperfections in your nature
that contradicted my perfect portrait.
It had been easier to gloss over the red flags
and pretend they weren't there
than to change this masterpiece I had created.

After a while, the painting's image had been distorted.
It cracked and chipped as our relationship worsened
with your lack of effort.
Your changing mood swings and insulting tones
were like harsh critiques of my artwork.
You're boring.
Are you not enjoying the exhibit
featuring the artwork that I've created for us?
Why do you keep asking me all these questions?
I'm sorry, I had no idea it was a problem.
I just wanted your opinion on these new ideas I wanted to paint.
I have a lot going on and I need some space.
You find my work so repulsive that you have to create
an excuse to not look at it.

Not being able to handle the critiques,
I started to paint myself in a better image.
An image that you would more readily accept.
It forced me to paint over my frown with a smile
and over the scars you've inflicted on my broken heart

MARY'AH "MO'ZART" ONWUKWE

so that it appears to be whole again.
With all this paint over me,
my personality hardened like a hollow statue.
No longer could I enjoy life through my colorful lenses
as I did before. I thought all you needed was a painter's touch
to make you just right,
just perfect for me.
But I failed to realize that art is only beautiful
in the eyes of the beholder.
And maybe that's why your beauty
only came from the canvas I painted you on.
You were never really beautiful inside
until I made you that way.
It's probably why I ignored those ugly parts of you
for so long. It's also why I refused to listen to outside critiques
of how my painting didn't match up to its reference.
I thought that there was no way for them to understand
my art since they didn't have my artistic eye.
They didn't get to see what I saw
when I placed my brush on the canvas.
Stroke by stroke, I floated away to a land
where it was just you and me,
no outside world trying to rip apart our unity.
Or maybe, my eyes staring at the canvas too long
caused me to hallucinate,
and paint what I wanted to see instead of reality.

DAYDREAMS & NIGHTMAREZ

CONTRADICTION

Why am I such a walking contradiction?
I love to lift weights and run on treadmills
but let water trickle from my brow or pits
and you've spoiled the fun for me.
Every year I make the same resolution
to shed off the thick coat I used to survive the winter,
yet I can't stop myself from saying "no"
to a bag of chips or cookies.
I manage to convince myself every time I need to get work done
that I can do it better from the comfort of my own bed,
and every time, the only thing that gets checked off
my to-do list is sleep. Each morning,
I complain about not getting enough beauty sleep,
yet each night, I tell myself one more episode
or chapter won't hurt. It always hurts, when am I gonna learn?
I press shuffle on my music playlist to only skip every song
that plays until it gets to one that I originally wanted to hear.
I speak all day about wanting to have a closer relationship
with God, but never open my Word enough,
so that we could have that one-on-one relationship.

MARY'AH "MO'ZART" ONWUKWE

When asked, "how are you?"
I always respond, "I'm good"
even when I know I am not.
I could be struggling with a problem and want your help,
yet will not open my mouth because I hate feeling
like I'm transferring my burden to you.
Even when people offer to help me with a problem,
I don't accept it because I can't admit that I'm not strong enough
to handle it on my own. Sometimes at night,
when I think everyone is asleep,
I lock my door and silently release the pains I've been holding in
all day, wishing that someone could notice how broken I am,
but as soon as someone knocks on the locked door,
I quickly dry my eyes and clear my throat to destroy
any evidence that would convict me of my brokenness.
I told a guy that I was cool with being his friend,
yet I've been in love with him for four years,
hoping that one day he'd notice.
I don't want to remember how he left me,
yet I keep memories of him, so I don't forget.
My pain is purposely hid behind a smile
and I have the nerve to get upset at others
when they can't see past my facade.
Why am I such a walking contradiction?

DAYDREAMS & NIGHTMAREZ

YOU HAD ONE JOB

You once told me that you'll provide me security,
but what should I do when your security makes me insecure?

You had one job: keep my heart safe,
yet you left it unguarded to the thieves in the night
and now it's your fault that it's been kidnapped.

You had one job: not to let my heart out of your sight
and now it's being beaten and abused
by its captor who calls themself: Depression.
It's being held for ransom, a ransom that I can't pay
because it'd cost me my life, so I had no choice,
but to allow my heart to be taken.

MARY'AH "MO'ZART" ONWUKWE

You had gotten distracted by the paparazzi of women who
swarmed around you looking to replace me and they succeeded
because you had one job and couldn't even complete it.
You allowed the tabloids of social media to dictate how you
should treat a woman and neglected your one responsibility.

You had one job: to protect my heart,
yet I see you with different women giving them the security
you we're supposed to give me.
When were you gonna tell me you changed jobs?
You left without a two weeks' notice
and now I'm vulnerable because your position is vacant
Who will protect my heart now?

You had one job and now I'm suffering
at the hands of an enemy that you'll never find.
Now, I'm left to wonder if I was ever good enough.
I'm left to wonder if I was worth enough for you to protect.
I'm left to wonder if you even noticed I was missing at all
because you had one job and failed.

FAILING GRADES

Have you ever felt like such a failure in life?

I have on more than one occasion.

If life was graded,

I'd have an F in relationships,

just because I could barely manage one,

let alone keep one.

The first relationship I had with a man failed because

he neglected his paternal obligations.

He abandoned me and kept telling me that he'd be back soon.

MARY'AH "MO'ZART" ONWUKWE

Lies, lies, lies.
They were all lies.
Now I cannot trust a thing a guy tells me.
I have fears of inadequacy and abandonment
that won't go away no matter how hard I try,
so, to start from a clean slate,
I graduated to dating any guy
who would pay me attention
which just so happened to be older guys.
Being a freshman in the dating scene, proved to be enjoyable.
I always thought my love to be like a breath of fresh air.
But sometimes, I clinged too tight to them,
and they began to suffocate
causing them to distance themselves from me.
This often activated my wounded and anxious inner child
which made me crazy in love.
Crazy enough to repeatedly call or text their phone
so that they wouldn't forget about me.
Crazy enough to follow all the women on their social media,
just to see if they were in another woman's likes and comments.
Crazy enough to randomly pop up at places they would
commonly frequent, just to coincidentally run into them.
The list could go on and on.
Maybe it's all my fault that I am alone right now.
The quest to find someone to love me more than I loved myself
made me desperate. Desperate enough to settle
for dudes cheating on me, blatantly lying to me,
and some even verbally abusing me before they abandoned me.

DAYDREAMS & NIGHTMAREZ

No amount of begging could make them stay
so, you can see why I failed in relationships.
This bad grade bled into other areas.

I had a D-minus in education.
This probably happened when I made men my major
instead of biology.
You would think starting my college career
with a couple scholarships
would be a big help in the right direction.
But it wasn't.
The class clowns I dealt with outside of school
had been too distracting so I lost my focus.
My grades in the classrooms reflected that.
After my first year in college,
one of the scholarships that paid most of my tuition
had been stripped from me.
Having to explain to my mother that she would now have to
cover the rest of my tuition out-of-pocket
was like being in the principal's office
as they list off every wrongdoing
that I've participated in to get to this point.
Not cool.
Nonetheless, I did better in school for a short while
before the next class clown repeated the cycle.
But this time, I managed to cover my tracks better
and slightly improve in my classes to avoid
another visit to the principal's office.

MARY'AH "MO'ZART" ONWUKWE

Skipping to junior year, I started to think about my future
of becoming an infectious disease doctor
and realized that I needed to speak to a guidance counselor
to discuss my next steps.
That was the stupidest idea of my life because the guidance
counselor almost guided me into a deep depression.
She told me that I should just kiss my dreams
of being a doctor goodbye because I would never make it
into medical school with my mediocre grades.
The existential crisis that followed made me want to just end life
but a talk with my mom restored my dreams
that were almost killed. It doesn't excuse the fact that
I am very well borderline failing in education.

The stress of failed relationships
and struggling through my education
really took a toll on my grade in health.
I had an F.
I had so many books in my bag
that contributed to carrying more weight,
weight that amounted to over 300 pounds.
Never in my life did I think it would reach such a number,
not only that but I suffer from sciatic back pain
from time to time due to carrying this heavy bag around.
It probably also caused me to suffer from
a mild form of bell's palsy. Thankfully that went away.
I am pre-fill-in-the-blank to a few medical conditions
but I never could stay committed to exercising

and eating healthy. I always had a see-food diet
where I saw the food and ate it.
Oftentimes more than I could actually eat.
It very much was triggered by school
and my failed relationships.
Emotional eating has been my savior to deal with my problems
instead of My Savior
and that's a reason why I'm also failing in religion.

My grade in religion is an F.
Not surprising, honestly.
I strayed from God because I wanted a relationship so bad
it became my sole focus,
not realizing that I really needed a relationship with God before
a relationship with an earthly man could ever survive.
I treated God like a genie
and discarded Him when I got my three wishes.
I'd pray for finances to help me get around
and buy food while on campus
and I never ended up stranded or hungry.
I repeatedly prayed to pass my classes
to avoid retaking them, and I would.
I always prayed for a companion
and when I got him, I stopped praying.
After each heartbreak, I would run back to God
with my head hanging low. He would welcome me back in
every time and I'd uphold my promise to solely focus on Him

MARY'AH "MO'ZART" ONWUKWE

until an attractive guy in my class gives me the slightest
attention and I'm fumbling and falling for him,
forgetting all about building with God.
I never read enough of God's textbook on how to live,
so, I failed every test He would give me.
It's probably why I had to repeat the same lesson
through so many different men.

Honestly, it's all my fault.
I'm the reason for my failing grades.
Who knows when I'll get my act together.

DAYDREAMS & NIGHTMAREZ

HIGH NOON

COMPLETED WORK

In Christ, we are a completed work.

It took me a while to really understand this concept.

Because how can I be a completed work

if I am still stumbling,

falling,

and failing in life?

Don't completed works need to be perfect?

The answer is no, they don't.

God is the author and finisher of our faith

and the beauty about being an author

is that the first time an author finishes a book

it's called a rough draft

because it's supposed to be rough.

MARY'AH "MO'ZART" ONWUKWE

Ya know, like the plot holes
that make you question your existence
and why you were even put on this earth.
The numerous grammar mistakes
that make you feel dumb for making it more than twice.
And the poor character development
that makes you wonder why you are so stagnant in your growth,
and why nothing is changing for you.
Those same books that authors cringe at
for seeming unfinished while claiming its completion,
can be revised,
and reworked,
even in its completed form
because an author knows how the book will end,
but there's always a surprise in the journey
that takes place to get there
as characters sometimes have a mind of their own.

Our lives are these books.
And we are the main characters of our books.
I mean haven't you ever wondered
why we call an end or start of a situation,
the end or beginning of a chapter in our lives?
Why even use the word "chapter" if our life isn't a book?
Don't chapters belong in books? They do.
So that means that the chapters that are in our living books
help us to tell stories that can breathe life into others, as stories
cannot live outside of their books.

DAYDREAMS & NIGHTMAREZ

It also means that each individual book has its own unique story
and God being the author and finisher of our faith
means that He is writing our stories all at once.

So, if you are getting this message,
then I need you to understand
that God isn't through with you yet.
If you are getting this message,
then I need you to understand
that He isn't finished writing your story.
Each new day that you live is a new page
being added to the book of your life,
so don't waste it.
Don't take for granted
each new page that gets added,
because it isn't promised to you.
Don't get too comfortable
because your conclusion
could come before this page runs out.

So, if God added a new page to the book of your life,
use it to get right with Him.
Use this page to go after the purpose
that He has placed in your heart
that you may still be trying to find.
Use this page to find it.

MARY'AH "MO'ZART" ONWUKWE

Use this page to start that business
that you've been wanting to start, but haven't,
because you underestimate your gift.
Use this page to go back to school
and finish or start a new education.
Use this page to get in touch
with the kids or parents
that you haven't talked to in a minute.
Use this page to forgive family members, or friends,
that have done something wrong to you that was so petty,
and so long ago because the hurt you are harboring inside
keeps you from moving on to true happiness.
Use this page to begin healing any traumas,
or hardships, you've encountered
throughout your story.
And whenever you feel like giving up, remember
that as long as you have a breath,
your story is still being written
and you are a completed work.

I MADE IT

Mama, I made it!
Four years of: constant tests, papers, and assignments;
struggling through coursework for my biology major
and excelling through coursework for my electives;
questioning if I chose the right college;
wondering if I should drop out altogether;
being in and out of relationships;
and shedding so many tears that I almost drowned in them.
But it's okay because...

I made it!
Despite losing a financial scholarship my first year;
several depressive episodes; having an existential crisis
which led to thoughts of giving up, not just in school, but in life;
failing a few more tests than I would have liked;
my GPA not being a 3.5 or above; and a school counselor
telling me my future in medicine was grim.

MARY'AH "MO'ZART" ONWUKWE

I made it!
And because I made it, I know that I can continue forward
to medical school. Despite the naysayers,
I turned my golden tassel from the right to the left
and earned a Bachelor's in Biology,
one of my greatest accomplishments in life.
I thank God for bringing me through.
I know that I can get into medical school despite my failures.
The journey may be longer, but I know I can make it with Jesus.
He gave me the desire to become a doctor
so, I know He'll open doors for me that no man can close.
I know I can do ALL things through Christ who strengthens me.
He's given me a wonderful support system
who has held me up when I felt weak.
I wouldn't have made it without them.

Just as I have made it, you can too!
Don't give up on your dreams and aspirations
because the journey ahead looks rough.
If those desires were placed in your heart,
just know that they were given to you for a reason.
Don't mind the people who tell you cannot do something.
They are the people who secretly know that you can do it,
they just don't want to see you succeed
because they are intimidated by your potential.
So, prove their worst fears right and go forth in your destiny.
I know you can make it!

DAYDREAMS & NIGHTMAREZ

THE PERFECT ANSWER

Okay class, our lesson has concluded, does anyone have any inquiries?

A hand raises and asks, how do we prevent our hearts from being filled with anxieties?

That is a wonderful question and one that is three-fold in nature. In order to answer it, I must first explain what a heart is which is major. The heart is a vessel that beats to keep us alive but the heart you speak of is not the most important for us to survive. The heart you speak of is the spiritual heart which isn't a heart at all but the mind. This was God's design when His Word tells us to Sanctify the Lord, God in our hearts. He wants us to do our part and create a special place for Him to reside in our thinking processes. It's how we can progress in life without the stress because as a man thinks in his heart, so is he. Your mouth speaks what your heart and mind are full of, whatever that may be. It's why your thinking process that encompasses your emotions and mannerisms, speak volumes as to who you are. So far, the first part of the answer has been given, so the second part is the meaning of the phrase, "let not your heart be troubled" which means to not be disturbed in your thinking bubble. Onto the third and final part of the answer, you need more of your mind and thinking process to be focused on Jesus, not less. Whatever you hold dearly to your heart, ask yourself if you grip God that way and you will get rid of a lot of your anxiety. When you grip onto God, nothing in this society can grip you. Take solace in the One who can grip you tight and secure you forever through every trial and test. The world has many distractions that can press their way in to control our spiritual hearts. This happens, in part, by us allowing these worldly pleasures and sin to take the throne of your minds instead of Jesus. Next.

A student who looked perplexed asks, how do we avoid being controlled by what we observe?

Great question and you avoid being controlled by learning how to reserve. Reserving judgment, actions, and speech before learning the facts can be a great start. In order to practice this, it would be smart to avoid going off first impressions. These indiscretions can often lead you to the wrong conclusions. These illusions are often why we allow our eyes to take the lead, and we fall in love with things and people that are draining and temporary. Instead, do your research to figure out all the facts that are necessary. You have to guard your heart as everything you do flows from it. There will be times where issues will come into your heart and mind and sit. If Jesus is sanctioned in your heart and mind, then He becomes the controlling factor of what stays and what goes. He prevents us from getting frozen in sin and destructive feelings because He screens the issue before it possesses you. He will allow you to absorb what is right and will cast out what is wrong before it even gets to you. When you allow the peace of God to rule in your heart, you will start to have a totally different point of view. Do not rely on your friends or outside sources for advice, instead, taking everything to God in prayer will suffice. Why settle for a resource when you can go directly to the Source for any answers you may seek? He is the only One who made you unique. Jesus is the same yesterday, today and forever. His love is open to whoever will receive Him. It is eternal and unchanging and will never dim. He loved us enough to die for us so trust in Him. It's not just enough to hear God's answer, but we must obey it, otherwise coming to Him for help would be pointless as we make our own decisions anyway and become joyless. The same logic can be applied to reading God's Word and not applying it to your reality. This will only lead you into situations that will have you questioning your morality. Okay, we have time for one more.

    Another hand raises and asks, so you said a lot about how we can endure any troubles that life throws at us, but where should our hope come from?

    I have the perfect answer that will sum up our class.
JESUS!

MARY'AH "MO'ZART" ONWUKWE

SEPARATE TO ELEVATE

Sometimes in life, you have to separate to elevate.
So that means getting rid of the dead weight
that is holding you down and holding you back
because you can't accelerate to your destination
if you have someone around you pushing the brake.
Sometimes it's better to be apart than together.
I understand that you two have
enjoyed many summer nights
and endured some harsh wintery weather without reason,
but some people were only meant to be
with you for a season.

DAYDREAMS & NIGHTMAREZ

And the time has come for the season to change.
Don't resist it, as I know you may want to.
This change is what'll help you grow.
Just have faith that once you let go,
you'll be able to fly to infinite heights,
and overcome the lowest depths.

Sometimes isolation isn't a bad thing.
Reverting to your solitude
is sometimes needed to regroup,
to collect your thoughts,
and to get yourself together.
If you find that once you reconnect,
that you two are on different paths,
then accept it.
Maybe it was destiny that you separated in the first place.
Because they can't go where you're going
and vice versa.
So, stop trying to drag people into your destiny
that is meant for you and you alone.
You will find yourself struggling to reach it
as you unnecessarily stack
their burdens and problems onto your shoulders
that only they were meant to carry.

Until you choose to depart,
you cannot start the process to repair your heart,
to find yourself again,

MARY'AH "MO'ZART" ONWUKWE

and to search for your one true purpose and calling.
It may be hard now, but future you
will commend you and be applauding you
for taking the first step in the right direction
to do what's best for you
in this moment.

So, the choice is yours.
I never mentioned any names,
but a person popped into your head, I'm sure.
You can stay where you are with this person
that you know isn't right for you,
remain stagnant,
and never truly be happy.
Or,
you can choose to have a peace of mind
in knowing that when you finally separate,
you'll begin to elevate.

DAYDREAMS & NIGHTMAREZ

SHINE, STAR, SHINE

When you wish upon a shining star,
do you recognize who you are?
and all that you could be?
Because you have been destined for greatness,
but it doesn't matter, if it's not something you can see.
This is what I learned from my second family,
my I Am Woke cast.

Coming up on our second performance of the play,
I started to eclipse my luminescence
because I couldn't imagine myself
being a star in the spotlight.
The asteroids of fear,
doubt, and insecurity

MARY'AH "MO'ZART" ONWUKWE

blocked me from believing in my ability.
Dark thoughts started to float around in my headspace like
I could never be as successful as the big names.
Who cares about little ole me?
I cannot fathom others wanting to
hear me speak my truth again,
because hardly anyone came to support me.
There is no way that I'm good enough
to perform my parts of this production.
What if I messed up badly and embarrassed myself?
I can't afford to disappoint anyone.

Gravity pulled down my confidence
like a meteorite crashing onto Earth.
The oxygen I needed to breathe depleted
as I became entrapped in a black hole
my thoughts created with no way to escape.
But, my cast,
my great I Am Woke cast,
heard my distress call and skyrocketed to my rescue.
They wrapped me in their kind words.
They spoke life into me.

They told me:
to keep working towards my goals and to keep writing
because the world needs this doctor for healing
but also needs to be healed through my words.

DAYDREAMS & NIGHTMAREZ

They told me:
my God-given talents weren't given to me haphazardly,
and that they were given to me because I had a purpose to fulfill
and that I needed to live in it truthfully
and wholeheartedly without restriction.

One of my first friends and mentors in poetry told me:
That I am what happens when preparation
meets opportunity: simply put,
a star.

A star that needed to shine to no limit
and allow myself to be free.
I hadn't realized it but the first night I've ever performed poetry,
January 14, 2022, was my big bang event.
Because ever since then,
Mo'zArt, the poet, spontaneously formed.

She is the other side of me
that I have to tap into to reach my full potential.
She is the one who kills it every time she steps onto stage.
She is the one who fears nothing
and takes risks in her art to reap the greatest rewards.
She is beautiful and has a colorful personality like a nebula,
and doesn't need anyone to tell her so.
She is the one who knows that she is perfectly
and wonderfully made,
and so are her words.

MARY'AH "MO'ZART" ONWUKWE

She is the one that has a gift to guide people
out of their dark matter using her shining light.
She is the one who has the gift to make people
whom she can't see, feel her words like magic,
or maybe it was stardust.
She became a motivation to the ones who are afraid
to step outside their comfort zone and blossom.
She is the one who won't dim her light,
just so that yours can shine brighter.
She's the one to tell you, "Respectfully, step ya game up."
And because Mo'zArt is all these things,
one beautiful soul from my family
helped me to realize that I, Mary'ah,
needed to step outta the way
when Mo'zArt is performing
so that she can have a place to shine
and take what's hers and she did just that
during the encore performance of I Am Woke.

The funny thing about stars is
that they are only really noticeable at night
in the darkest times,
yet they don't disappear during the brightest days.
They don't stop shining because of the sun,
instead, they are concealed by it.
Since I am a star, I too,
am concealed by the Son…
of God

DAYDREAMS & NIGHTMAREZ

as He shines through me and shines brighter than I.
Because without Him, who am I?
Nobody.
Because greater is He that is in me,
than he that is in the world.
So, when you see me and my luminescence,
understand that it's not just positivity that you should see,
but the Heavenly Father that resides in me
that is shining through any fears, or doubts,
that may try to overcome me
and burst my confidence like a supernova.
For my God,
did not give me the spirit of fear
but of power,
of love,
and of a sound mind.
And with this power,
I step into my boldness, declaring my truth.
With this love,
my heart can bleed onto this open canvas,
hoping that you'll feel me.
With this sound mind,
I will not question my worth, or capability
ever again.

My second family always told me
about how I completed them and balanced everyone out, almost
like I had been cosmically designed that way.

MARY'AH "MO'ZART" ONWUKWE

My second middle name is one with an Igbo origin.
It's Adazuonu,
in which Ada means first daughter
and zuonu means to complete.
I am the one to complete any family
that I've become a part of,
any project that I've started,
and any goal that I've made.

So, when I wish upon a shining star,
I will finally recognize who I am
and all that I can be.
I am no longer blind to the bright future
I see in my destiny.
A star shining in her own light
determined not to let anyone,
not even herself,
dim her luminescence.
So, that even if there are dark days, or bright nights,
she will keep reminding herself
to shine, star, shine.

FULL MOON

IS IT ME?

Is it me or am I just very easy to abandon?
Or did I chase them away?
Does my personality lack luster?
Do I shine too bright?
Am I toxic?
Am I too nice?
Did I apologize one too many times?
Did I ask too many questions?
Do I cry too much?
Do I not express my feelings at all?
Do I cling too much to your words that leave me hanging?
Is it me?

MARY'AH "MO'ZART" ONWUKWE

Am I that sore on the eyes?
Do all my curves and crevices offend you?
Am I not good enough to show off proudly to the world?
Or was I only good enough for your bed?
Is it me?

Did I give too much too easily?
Was it my lack of boundaries
and self-esteem that turned you off?
Or did my insecurities
and constant need for reassurance do the trick?
Is it me?

Why do I keep building up men for other women
when I have no real estate or contractor licenses?
Why is it her and not me?
Was I not enough for you?
Or am I just not enough of her?
Did you actually like the traits that I possess?
Or did you just wish they were attached to someone else?
Is it me?

Is there something wrong with me? There has to be
if I still wake up alone, right?
If everyone has their happily ever after already,
then it's gotta be me, right?
Why can't it be me?
I wish it was me.

DAYDREAMS & NIGHTMAREZ

WHY AM I SO DIFFERENT?

Why am I so different?
Why don't I get the princess treatment?
I deserve to have my doors opened for me,
to be catered to,
to want for nothing,
yet, I get treated like trash, like hand-me-downs.
I get passed around and tossed away as if I meant nothing.
I get treated like cold McDonald's fries when I should
get treated like fresh-out-the-grease Chick-fil-a fries.
I get treated like candy corn and never like pink starbursts.

Why is it so easy for them to do the right thing for the next girl
and I'm stuck as the guinea pig to see how many stale excuses
they can feed to a girl before she gets fed up?
It's not fair. I didn't ask to be played,
cheated on, and used because you weren't ready to love
and then magically, you are when the next girl comes along.

MARY'AH "MO'ZART" ONWUKWE

Why am I so different?
Why do I get broken
versions of you when the next girl gets healed
parts? Or did you have the potential all along and refused
me access to it? Why am I always cunningly lied to
and the next girl gets the unfiltered truth?
I always have to beg for the bare minimum
and the next girl gets spoiled with your full participation
without uttering a word.

I deserve to feel like I am a priority,
yet when it comes to me, I am put on the backburner.
Scratch that.
I'm not even on the stove.
Because when our relationship, or rather situationship,
gets too hot, you go ghost. Why am I gassed up to be consumed
by a guy that wanted me first?
I understand that I am very intelligent and in school,
I understand that I have a lot of drive and ambitions to achieve,
along with creative talents,
I understand that I believe in God, attend church often,
and center Him in my life
and that all these things may intimidate you.
But why am I so different?

Yes, I understand that I am called out to be apart from the world
and not in it, but does that mean I deserved to get treated
less than? How many of these men are gonna be lessons?

DAYDREAMS & NIGHTMAREZ

When will the day come that a guy comes into my life
to be a blessing? I am so sick of getting treated like a commoner
or peasant when I treat you like royalty.
You serve me your spare breadcrumbs
that would initially have me satiated then leave me starving
while you give the next girl an entire bakery.
I don't deserve to get treated so different when I sacrifice
my all out of my love for you. In the end,
you would claim that you never wanted my love.

How can you promise me the world and break it,
yet give the next girl a galaxy? Do I not deserve
to be among the stars? Why am I always kept in the dark
and a secret yet the next girl is kept in the spotlight
as you show her off in your arms?
I only get shown your house or your car.
Why don't I get taken out on a real date in a public place?
How come I could never get you to support my dreams
and passions, yet you are the main cheerleader
on the next girl's dream team?
Why does the next girl receive the daydreams I've had about us,
and I get the nightmares of you breaking my trust over
and over
and over again?

Why am I so different? Why am I so hard to love?
I have yet to find the love that I have been searching for.

MARY'AH "MO'ZART" ONWUKWE

The guys that come into my life give me that love for a trial,
but never let me buy a subscription.
I never had a guy be real with me.
They always tell me that they want a down chick, a ride or die,
somebody that's loyal who will stick by his side.
They failed to tell me that it meant sticking through the BS.
Cheating, ghosting, etcetera etcetera.
Why is it so hard for me to find genuine love? Even platonic.
Guys don't befriend me for the sole purpose of being my friend.
They do so with hopes
that one day, I'll invite them into my bedroom.

Why am I so different?
Why am I not chosen?
Was I even a choice to you?
Do I deserve this?
I shouldn't be treated so differently, so why am I?

DAYDREAMS & NIGHTMAREZ

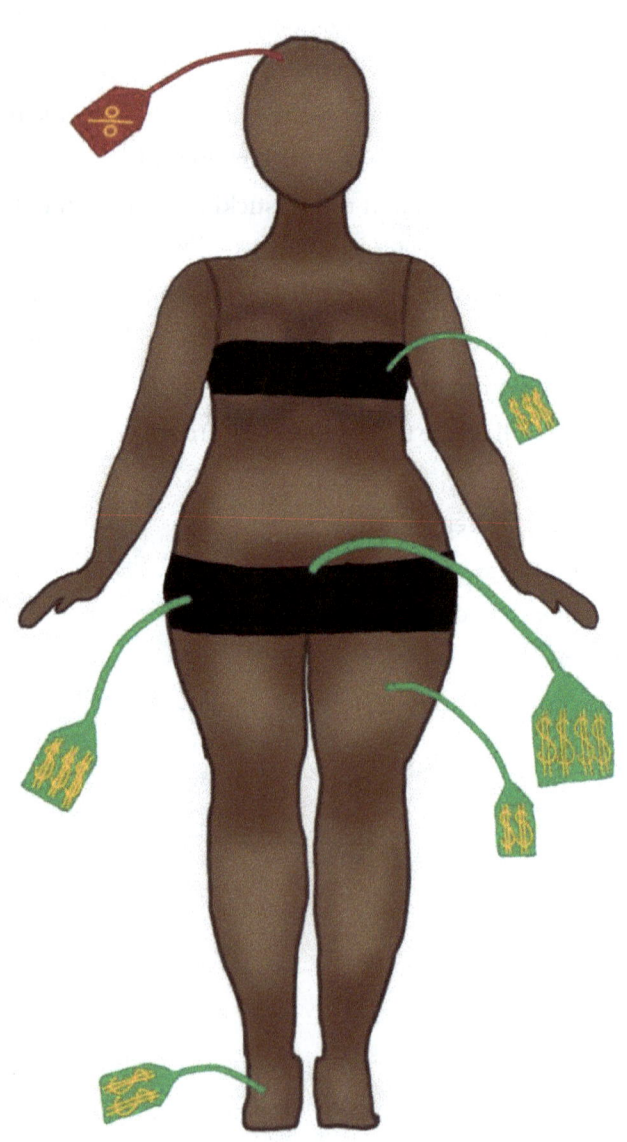

MARY'AH "MO'ZART" ONWUKWE

IS THAT ALL I'M WORTH?

When you look at me, what do you see?
Do you see a respectable young black woman?
Or just a heavy chest and a plump behind?
Odds are you only saw the latter half.
Did you even hear me speak at all?

By now, you'd think I'd be used to it.
I'd been receiving this type of attention
from the ripe age of sixteen. The tenth grade.
I'm now twenty-two and have just graduated college.
I've endured six or more years of sexual harassment,
whether physical or verbal, because let's be honest,
this probably started earlier,
that is just when I started to notice.

For example,
grown men staring me up and down in the market
or as I'm crossing the street.
Others in cars catcalling when no cats are around to be called.
It terrified me so much when I was younger.
Young boys in high school snickering behind me
about how they captured a picture of my butt.
Did they not know I could hear them?
Other young boys in an overcrowded lunch line
punching my behind because they wanted to see it jiggle.
Despicable.
Is that all I'm worth?

DAYDREAMS & NIGHTMAREZ

A fat butt and big boobs, is that all that matters?
Not the fact that I now have a degree in Biology,
and plan to become an Infectious Disease Doctor.
Or should I just forget that I can write impactful poetry and
imaginative novels, and draw picture perfect portraits,
all because my body curves in more places than most?
Do I not add value with these added attributes
of my personality and God-given gifts?
Or is it the fact that my God-given curves
are too much for your hollow brain to absorb and process,
let alone my talents and character?
Is that all I'm worth?

Mark me off with a price tag.
I'm only worth as much as my body can produce.
Is my body the only thing I can use to pay for your attention?
Why should I have to sell myself to you
and you have nothing to offer?
Are you not interested in having my mind?
Are you not interested in learning about my heart
and what it takes to love me?
Maybe not, because maybe my body is all I'm worth to you.

When guys look at me, they don't see someone they can respect
because the first thing out their mouth
has something to do with sex.
The number of guys that have approached me with sex
on their tongue is disgusting.

MARY'AH "MO'ZART" ONWUKWE

They reeked of audacity to feel comfortable enough
to speak to me in such a way,
especially after just meeting me.
My body causes men to act in a frenzy
with their one-track mind,
which will never work to win me over, because I am a maze.
Your one-track mind will have you hitting a wall
as my interest in you becomes lost, never to be found again,
if you even held it in the first place.
Because did I ask you for that?
Did I ask for unsolicited pictures of your manhood?
Do I have "easy to smash" etched on my forehead or something?
Do I have "Friends with Benefits"
sneakily tattooed somewhere on my body?
Do you think I deserve to be objectified and disrespected,
because my body has hills and valleys in the right places?
Did it ever occur to you that I wanted to be seen
for more than just my body?
Did I vocalize that I wanted you
between my thighs?
Is sex with me all that matters?
Is that all I'm worth?

People tell me all the time, "I wish I had a booty like yours!"
Yes, yes, but this booty like mine
can't find someone worthy of my time,
because all the guys that approach me want one thing:
to get inside these jeans.

DAYDREAMS & NIGHTMAREZ

This sex-crazed generation
doesn't want the Love Jones kind of love that I'm craving.
Is it too much to ask for a guy
to want to learn the person inside of me
without wanting to get inside of me?
I can't help, but feel that I am worth more,
but guys don't want to look deep enough
without wanting to go deep enough.
I can't call you mine in public,
but I bet you'd love for me to say that I'm all yours
when the lights dim.
I'm just reduced to late night calls,
and the bare minimum.
I'm just reduced to a piece of meat that men stare at
as if they are waiting to devour me.
I do not flaunt my body nor show excessive skin.
Yet, I'm gawked at in a way that makes me feel naked.
Is that all I'm worth?

This inward woman can't be worth much at all
because she is undervalued.
No one sees her importance.
No one cares.
I'm just a big girl with big dreams,
but all they can see are my big thighs.
Yes, thick thighs save lives,
but these thick thighs don't save me from the lies
that are told to get between them.

MARY'AH "MO'ZART" ONWUKWE

I wonder how many women have fallen for your tricks
to make you think you can get away with it---again.
But you are sadly mistaken silly rabbit,
because your tricks ain't fooling the kid.
And that isn't all that I'm worth!

DAYDREAMS & NIGHTMAREZ

UGLY DUCKLING

I wish I wasn't such an ugly duckling.
Nobody wants to love me.
Nobody wants to be around me.
Nobody thinks I'm beautiful.
Nobody realizes my worth but mother duck,
when she's been around.
She's helped me with the harsh feelings, and I thank her for it,
but when I'm out in the world by myself,
it's hard to keep those same messages
in the forefront of my mind.
Because the world doesn't treat me this way.
The world treats me as if I am ugly.
Maybe I am.

MARY'AH "MO'ZART" ONWUKWE

I'm not a duckling that could get hundreds or thousands of likes
on Instagram just by posting my face alone.
I'm a conventionally unattractive duckling.
I don't meet society's standards of beauty.
I have dark skin and feathers.
The hair on my head is short, and kinky, and 4C.
My short and stout body and limbs
are big and lumpy in all the wrong places.
Nobody values my natural features.
Nobody cares.
The idea of the natural body has become obsolete as it degrades
into the cold streams of insecurity and comparisons
that my mind now swims in.
I shiver from all the self-hate that is seeping into my body.
My brother and sister ducklings who are deemed worthy
of society's approval, I silently envy,
because I cannot relate to them.
I cannot be them.

I am the ugly duckling that male ducklings
never reference when hanging out with my friends.
I am the ugly duckling that only gets recognized
if a male duckling wants a two-piece of these thighs.
I am the ugly duckling that will remain forever alone.
I am an ugly duckling
so, I guess that's why I don't deserve love.
I guess that's why I'll never find it.

DAYDREAMS & NIGHTMAREZ

I know that my Father has created me
to be wonderfully and beautifully made in His image
so does that mean my Father thinks I'm ugly too
to have created me in such a way?
Does it mean that He didn't care
to spend much time creating me
if I turned out to be such an ugly duckling?
I can only hope that one day
I'll turn into a beautiful swan, but it's hopeless
to hope. Some things are just too ugly to repair.

MARY'AH "MO'ZART" ONWUKWE

PICK ME

Pick me, pick me, pick me,
that's what I've been screaming at you for years,
yet my words fall upon deaf ears
so, it made sense as to why you couldn't hear me
pleading my case of how we would be the perfect couple
if you just gave us a chance.
You turned a blind eye so that you couldn't see me
trying so hard to be noticed by you.
Couldn't you feel, by my attachment to your rib,
that I wanted you to pick me
like God picked Eve from Adam?
You said you like me for who I am,
but you don't really like me for who I am

because if you did, I'd be enough for you.
You wouldn't search for the qualities that I possess
in other women when you could just have me.
I've come to the conclusion that you would rather
suffer at the hands of women playing with your heart
than to allow yourself to be loved by me.
These women didn't even pick you
and you still choose them. I pick you every time.
I guess my choice doesn't matter.

You give to women who don't even deserve
a drop of your affection, an entire ocean of it
and they misuse and abuse you.
They instead, used the ocean you gave them to drown you
because you can't swim.
Every time.
And who's always there to throw you a buoy
when your heart is heavy, and you are suffocating
on the consequences of your own actions?
Me.
Every time.
You would thank me for saving you and immediately go to
search for someone else to be your new safe haven
and the cycle repeats. Why won't you just pick me?
We would literally be the most perfect match in the universe.
We have a connection out of this world
that I'm still struggling to find in other people.
I know you feel it. You told me

MARY'AH "MO'ZART" ONWUKWE

you felt it. So why can't you pick me?
We could talk about anything.
Our conversations could jump from serious
to goofy
to intellectual
to spiritual
and repeat effortlessly.
I am the only woman you've invited into the innermost sanctum
of your mind to allow me to know
your darkest secrets and biggest sins
that you haven't told a soul about,
but me.
I am the only woman you can talk freely with
about your loudest, most troublesome thoughts
because I am the only woman that can quiet the noise
and put your mind at ease.
How could you not pick me?

I was so desperate to be picked I unknowingly allowed myself to
be your side piece. The piece you would break off whenever
your girlfriend wasn't around.
You told me so many times you would leave her.
I kept reassuring myself that once you left her,
you would surely come to your senses
and pick me. You told me
you had feelings for me and that you cared about me
so, I played my part and waited on the sidelines
for my special day to come.

DAYDREAMS & NIGHTMAREZ

I became the woman you Facetimed and chilled with
while your girlfriend worked.
The sneaky link
that gave her body to you as an offering of her love
because she had already given you her heart
and you rejected it.
I never once cared about hurting that woman's feelings
as I devoured pieces of you that I should've never tasted.
Guilt and shame didn't convict me of my sins
because my desire for wanting you to pick me
had been greater,
much greater.
You never left her while I became a jezebel.
How stupid could I have been to think
that you would pick me
over her? It was never going to be me.
Why did I want you to pick me so bad?
Why do I *need you* to pick me?

You dropped me like our bad habits.
Now I beg for sleep to pick me.
Yet I'm spending all my nights reminiscing on good times
and crying right after.
I beg my appetite to pick me.
But food doesn't taste as sweet as your kisses,
so, there's no point in insulting my tastebuds.
I beg for a peace of mind to pick me.
But you were my peace, and now you're gone,

so, I can't help but to be conflicted.
All I wanted to be was chosen by you.
Upon self-reflection, I realized that I wasn't even a choice,
not even an option. Never once
did you consider picking me.

Many nights blurred together as they passed
and I lay awake in bed numb to the world.
A notification on my phone catches my attention.
It's a memory from my photo app
with a picture of you and me.
Clicking on it, I stare at it for what seems like eternity.
One bolded question appeared in my head:
Why did I try so hard to be picked by you for so long?
One italicized answer followed it:
Never once did I pick myself.

DAYDREAMS & NIGHTMAREZ

GOLDEN HOUR

DAYDREAMS & NIGHTMAREZ

YOUR CHOICE

While I screamed *pick me, pick me, pick me,* to the men
I've encountered in my life, I never once stopped
to listen to You saying, *I chose you.*
So, I always questioned why I was never picked,
failing to recognize that the answer
was that I had already been chosen.
Before I came to You, before I was
conceived in my mother's womb,
and before the foundation
of the world, You chose *me.*
Many people don't get to be chosen by You
or come to know You.
But you saw fit to pick a sinner such as I,
to be one of your children.

MARY'AH "MO'ZART" ONWUKWE

A thought that I still find hard to fathom.
You thought of me way before I ever thought of myself.
I know that guys did not pick me because I was worthless.
It had nothing to do with that
and everything to do with You already laying claim to me.
You knew that I wouldn't have given You the time of day
had You allowed the distractions under the sun to set
because I have a form of spiritual ADD
where I am focused on You one moment
and then become lost in the world the next. You would find me
and want a relationship so that You could refine me
and build me up to step into my purpose.
And I, time and time again, resisted
because I had become so fixated
on finding the love I lost from my father
when I should've spent more time with You
to get the love I needed from my Father.
Forgive me for not appreciating being Your Choice.

When I struggled with sins of the flesh,
making me wretched and undone
You still loved me and chose me to be one
of yours. I don't deserve the mercy and grace you give.
Even when my shame makes me want to hide from You,
You play my game of hide-n-seek and still choose me.
You tell me that my choice to serve You
and believe in You isn't even my choice
because You chose me to have a mind to serve and believe.

DAYDREAMS & NIGHTMAREZ

I could not come to this on my own.
I was dead in sin, and You walked amongst the graveyard
to save me by name. Now I have an everlasting life through You.
You have the authority. You said let there be light,
and there was
light. Your Light
that shines on me in my life and through me.
Never again will I complain about not being chosen by a man
because You have chosen me
and I am Yours.

SHAMEFUL TO SHAMELESS

Shame is a powerful feeling.
According to the Oxford dictionary,
shame is a painful feeling of humiliation or distress
caused by the consciousness of wrong or foolish behavior.
I have shame.

It can be more easily recognized
as balls and chains being wrapped
around my waist and each foot.
Each step is calculated as the sound of my sins
scraping the floor haunts me.
Too much shame has accumulated after many years of sin.
Too much to carry and now my hands are full.

DAYDREAMS & NIGHTMAREZ

I am shameful.
My mind is shackled to the thoughts
that God doesn't want to be bothered by such an unclean child,
so, I cannot bear approaching His Holy Throne.
Day by day, I disgust myself more and more
because the shame that I carried covered my reflection
when I looked in the mirror.
Despite this, each day I would still sin
because I strayed so far from God
that I felt it would be pointless to return to Him now
in my messy state. Conviction pounded more harshly
on my heart, the farther I strayed,
making the shame that much heavier to carry.

All this shame made me run farther from God
than towards Him because I am unworthy.
I don't deserve to be called His.
The more I ran, the wearier I became.
I found my stride shortening as my legs could barely lift
until I was forced to stop.
Dropping the weights, I bent over to catch my breath,
and saw two pairs of feet.
One belonged to me, turning my head to see
whom the other set of feet belonged to,
I see that they belonged to the Lord.

He stood with open arms and a sympathetic smile
ready to accept me again.

MARY'AH "MO'ZART" ONWUKWE

I burst into tears and hugged my Father, apologizing profusely.
He wrapped His arms of love around me and comforted me
by saying, *"I forgive you*
and have thrown your sins into a sea of forgetfulness
to remember them no more.
My Son died for your sins, and they have been atoned for.
I don't hold any of your sins against you.
I know it is because of the flesh that you are in.
You're stumbling doesn't make Me love you any less.
I know the enemy may have tricked you into believing that
and that's why you tried to run from Me.

But My Love for you will never fade as you are My Child.
Little did you know, I was running alongside you the entire time,
waiting for you to get tired of running,
and come back to Me.
Please remember that when you are weak,
I am strong.
You can always cast your cares upon Me
and I will give you rest.
I can help you become stronger than the sins
and problems you have faced. If you will allow Me to operate on you,
then I can begin to help you heal from past hurts and traumas
so that you can evolve into the person I've always known you could be.
There is no reason to carry around this shame."

With a flick of the wrist, He breaks every chain
and shame releases its shackles from me.

DAYDREAMS & NIGHTMAREZ

I felt my spirits lift and joy replenished my soul.
Because of my Savior, I have no more shame tied to me.
Because of my Savior, I am shameless.

MARY'AH "MO'ZART" ONWUKWE

DIAMOND IN THE MUD

I am a diamond.
A diamond, by definition, is a precious stone
consisting of a clear and colorless crystalline form
of pure carbon, the hardest naturally occurring substance.
Yea, that sounds about right.
I am precious.
My transparency, and realness,
come from my pure carbon heart.
And that's the hardest thing about me
because it's rare, that you'll find another like mine.

Diamonds are formed under intense heat and external pressure.
Forming a diamond could take a few days, months,
or even several million years.
You wanna know a secret?
I didn't always know I was a diamond.
I actually believed I was a rhinestone,
a piece of cut glass that's meant to imitate a diamond.
How did I come to believe this?

DAYDREAMS & NIGHTMAREZ

It's a simple explanation really.
I surrounded myself with people,
especially guys, who thought they could tell the difference.
Because I didn't know my worth,
I let them tell me who and what I was.
It was fitting, because they treated me like a rhinestone,
like I was worthless and easily replaceable.
I had been treated this way for so long,
that I believed that I was,
because people treat items of value with care, caution, and love.
They are gentle because they don't want to damage it.
Yet with me, I had been covered with dirt,
so that I couldn't see my own beauty.
And spit on, so that I felt disgusted with myself
for even thinking that I deserved better.
This mud that was smeared across my identity
made it easy for them to be reckless with me
as they stomped on me, tossed me around,
and chipped away at my self-worth
before they left me.

It was in my hours of darkness and loneliness,
that I started to shine. The light inside of me
began to seep through the cracks in the mud.
It wasn't until my Heavenly Father took me in His Hands
and washed away the mud of other's opinions
of whom I was supposed to be,
that I could really glisten in His Holy Light.

MARY'AH "MO'ZART" ONWUKWE

I started to see that something was different about me,
different within me.
Rhinestones can't withstand much pressure, or heat, at all.
In fact, they crack and break.
It was then, that I realized that I had been misinformed.

I was no rhinestone, just a diamond in the mud.
It took me twenty-two years to come to that realization.
I learned that people treating me less than what I was worth
didn't mean that I was worth-less.
I learned that I had to recognize my worth
because my worth won't always be recognized by others.
And that even if others cannot see the value that I possess,
it doesn't mean that I am placed at a lesser value.
It simply means that I was never meant to be seen
through their cheap lenses.

I am invaluable as my worth
does not come with a price.
It cannot be bought with money, or rhinestone gestures
that are made to imitate a diamond kind of love.
I am precious and deserve to be treated as such.
I am to be handled with the utmost care and concern.
Now that I know my worth,
I won't go back to being a diamond in the mud,
but a diamond that will shine in all seasons
radiating God's Love.

DAYDREAMS & NIGHTMAREZ

WHO AM I?

If you ask me who I am, I'll answer
that I am not thee I am that I am.
I am my Father's Child
and I do not speak of the mortal kind.
This Father that gave birth to the Son that resides in me.
This Father who created the land and the sea.
This Father sent me.

I am the one who walks in her destiny
whose purpose is to plant the seed, so that it can be
watered and nurtured to help you grow.
I am the one who is learning to heal herself
so that she can heal others through her gifts of the Spirit.
In and through her art,
she shares pieces of herself which have
pieces of Him that she can gift to you

MARY'AH "MO'ZART" ONWUKWE

so that you may piece back together
your heart, if it's broken,
and your life, if it's been fragmented.
I am filled with the Light that shines in the darkness.
A light that the darkness could never put out,
no matter how hard it tried.
I am the shining north star to help guide you to freedom
from the shackles of sin. I am not perfect,
but I strive every day to be like the One that is.

DAYDREAMS & NIGHTMAREZ

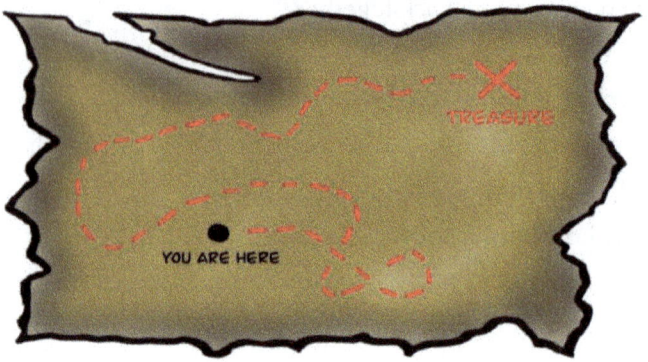

HIDDEN TREASURE

I've been hidden in plain sight against my will.
I've been hidden and I want to be found.
I am sick and tired of being overlooked, underpaid,
and unrecognized while my equals are living lavishly
and comfortably with everyone's eyes on them.
When will it be my turn to reap the blessings I'm owed?

A soft voice whispers in my spirit, *"Patience. Trust my timing."*
I know, I know that I should move to fulfill Your Will
and not my own
but why couldn't I have gotten a warning
that I am being hidden?
The voice answers back,
"Because you would have resisted like you are now."
It's hard knowing that I am gifted
and that I am heavily anointed, and I am being covered,
shielded from the outside world, so they don't notice me yet.

MARY'AH "MO'ZART" ONWUKWE

Feelings of self-doubt and worthlessness snake their way in
and I began to wonder if I am truly as great as I think I am,
if I even have the skills necessary to perform the desires
placed in my heart because nobody recognizes me.
Nobody sees me
because I have been hidden.
The same voice speaks again and says,
"My thoughts are not your thoughts.
My ways are not your ways.
Please listen as I tell you that I hide you for two reasons:
to protect you and to prepare you.

You are precious to Me, My Child. A treasure
that I have to hide to protect you from pirates and vultures
who seek to lie to, steal from, and destroy you
while hiding behind a smile you can't see as fake.
You are too quick to accept the outer appearance
people show you at face value
instead of using the gift I've given you of discernment
to realize that the guy you claim is an angel sent from Me
is really hiding his demons behind his smile.
Demons that will only give you hell on earth.
You think that there's no one in this world who can love you,
but that is false. I am hiding you from the suitors around you
because I value you and I know that they will not.
You experienced this one too many times and I didn't hide you then
because I needed you to want to get tired of chasing men
who cannot give you the love that you desire, all on your own.

DAYDREAMS & NIGHTMAREZ

And after many attempts, the fix you got
from these temporary relationships did not have the same effect
because you started to want more for yourself.
Your standards started rising.
And when you gravitated towards leaving those enticing devils alone,
I had to make sure they couldn't find you again
to disrupt your process of getting to know Me
so, I hid you in my secret place from the conspiracies of man.

I hide you to protect you from you.
You can be easily distracted, My Child.
I had to remove you from environments
that will take your attention away from Me.
And even then, you still tried your hardest to be seen and heard.
You get upset when nobody pays you any attention.
It is because I have closed off their ears and covered their eyes.
The attention you seek to be noticed, comes with a price.
Being out in the open means that everyone can see you
and has access to you,
even the ones who don't deserve it.
I hide you so that the only people who can find you
are ones that come to Me for directions.
You must learn, My Child, to move in silence.
Too many people knowing all your moves
can halt your progress and growth.
They can dismantle the character that I am building in you.
I hide you to protect you, not to punish you.
This season of hiding is not meant to feel like a prison.

MARY'AH "MO'ZART" ONWUKWE

You would know that if you spent more time with Me
instead of wallowing in your loneliness and insecurities.

I hide you to prepare you for the next season I plan to elevate you to.
During this season, I have to do a work in you
so that when I elevate you, I can do a work through you.
I have to build your character to be equipped to handle the new season.
As I elevate you, your enemies will also elevate in power to try
and knock you off your post.
I need time to cultivate a strength in you
so that as you encounter obstacles,
you won't succumb to the tricks of the enemy.
I need you to become comfortable with being alone.
As I elevate you, more and more people will fall away from you
because they cannot go where I am taking you.
You will have more people rooting against you than supporting you.
I need you to be able to validate yourself
and realize your worth and identity in Me.
I need you to recognize who you are
so that no one can tell you any different.
I need you to walk in confidence that I am that I am
and I have sent you to complete a task for Me.

I am hiding you to prepare you for your blessing
so that you don't mishandle it because you are not yet ready.
You are wondering why you aren't eating from the fruits of your
harvest, well, my child, it's because you haven't been sowing the right
seeds. There are some issues that I need you to stop running from

and face, so that you can heal.
Therefore, I hide you to take my time in presenting each issue that you
need to overcome because you would become overwhelmed
if I brought them all up at once.
The blessing I have for you is waiting for you.
It's yours and no one can take it from you.
Believe it or not, you prolong your blessing by remaining stagnant.
So please don't shy away from the tasks I have called you to do
because they seem too great. I know exactly who you are
and the capabilities that you have.
I know exactly why I selected you
to do what you will in your next season.
I make no mistakes.
I am a patient God and need you to develop the same virtue.
If you have a little faith as small as a mustard seed,
it can move mountains and take you to Heaven.
But if you can manage to have a great faith,
it can bring Heaven to you.
You must learn to trust me and my timing
because my timing is best.

This new season requires a new you.
You must crucify the old parts of you daily
and renew your spirit to handle the obstacles you may face.
You must also pass the tests I give you in this season of obscurity.
I will allow people and objects into your life
that you have once fallen victim to,
to see if your reaction to it has changed,

so, that I can be sure that you are truly ready
to be unveiled to the world.
Until then, you cannot advance to your next season
and I will not let you be found.
I do my best work in isolation,
so, if I have to spend more time cultivating you in this season,
then so be it because I love you, My Child
and would never do anything to harm you.
Please remember that you are hidden because your worth
to Me is incomprehensible
and more than you could ever imagine.
Trust the process and treasure it."

DAYDREAMS & NIGHTMAREZ

LAST QUARTER

MONSTERS

Loneliness.
It's the crippling feeling that claws its way into my life
and eats me up at night. Its razor-sharp teeth
sink deep into my identity and self-worth
and dismember its strong core.
The stench of my bleeding soul
attracts more of the pack as loneliness never travels alone.
Depression and anxiety join in as my heart slows.
It's not the monsters under my bed
that I needed to worry about, but the ones that lingered
deep inside my head, whispering to me
that my presence on this earth

MARY'AH "MO'ZART" ONWUKWE

is wasted space

because no one notices when I'm absent.

In fact, if my presence

truly made a difference

in people's lives,

it wouldn't have been so easy

for them to leave me

without a defense

to battle these monsters

and their harassment.

DAYDREAMS & NIGHTMAREZ

SHATTERED

Step. Back.
Stay. Away.
Don't come any closer.
Behind the yellow tape please.
It's for your own protection.
This is a crime scene,
and you don't want to disturb the evidence.
The evidence of someone's brokenness breaking me.
The jagged shards of their brokenness have punctured me
and now have made a permanent residence inside me.

I know it wasn't intentional
because they said they loved me.
Oh, how I wish their love could superglue
my broken pieces back together.
Oh, how I wish their love was gentle enough

to remove their broken shards from me.
But alas, their love wasn't authentic, so instead of healing me,
it was their accomplice abetting them in tearing me apart.
They didn't catch me as I fell for them, or had I been tripped?
Their hollow I love you's now sting
like salt had been poured on my open wounds.

I am now a threat to anyone around me.
I am now hazardous material
that needs to be contained behind this yellow tape.
So, don't come any closer.
I am now marked dangerous.
I was once labeled fragile.
But someone's son wasn't too careful
with my packaging, so now,
the glass shards of my being are exposed.

Stop shining your lights in my face.
Please!
No flash photography or recording—
Please!
This is a private matter, not to be exploited on every tabloid.
You'll damage me more.
The light only reminds me of how shattered I am.
And I am tired of looking at me.

Step back!
Stay away!

DAYDREAMS & NIGHTMAREZ

For I am shattered, and I don't want you to get cut
on my broken pieces. Broken pieces
that are too painful to remove, so healing isn't an option.
The blood that trickles down my frame is not only mine,
but also, the blood of those who have tried to help me.
Their blood stains the jagged shards of what I used to be.

The guilt of cutting them now haunts my dreams
because I wasn't quick enough to stop them.
I wasn't strong enough to say,
"No, I got it!"
I wasn't compassionate enough to tell them,
"I'm only gonna hurt you. So, please stay away."
No, I let them risk themselves for me
because I didn't want to be shattered anymore.
I didn't want these pieces of other people's brokenness
breaking me anymore. But they were all vain attempts
as the glass shards remained and only sank deeper into me
slicing me open wider and creating bigger wounds
while those who tried to help me,
now have their own trauma to heal from.

So, heed my pleas
and remain behind the yellow tape.
It's not safe for you.
I can't be the reason
for another broken person breaking people,
just as a broken person broke me.

MARY'AH "MO'ZART" ONWUKWE

Now when the yellow tape is lifted,
and the evidence is all collected.
It will be examined,
and they will find
that the main culprit...
is me.

I confess that I had been warned
as I have warned you.
My glass shards breed loneliness.
I can't be responsible for spreading it more
than I have already done.
So, if solitude and suffering is my life sentence,
then, I accept it.

They told me
that they would hurt me
in more ways than one.
But I had been too naive to comprehend.
I couldn't read between the lines.

Maybe it had been in the fine print.
And by the time I got close enough to read it,
it had already been too late.

DAYDREAMS & NIGHTMAREZ

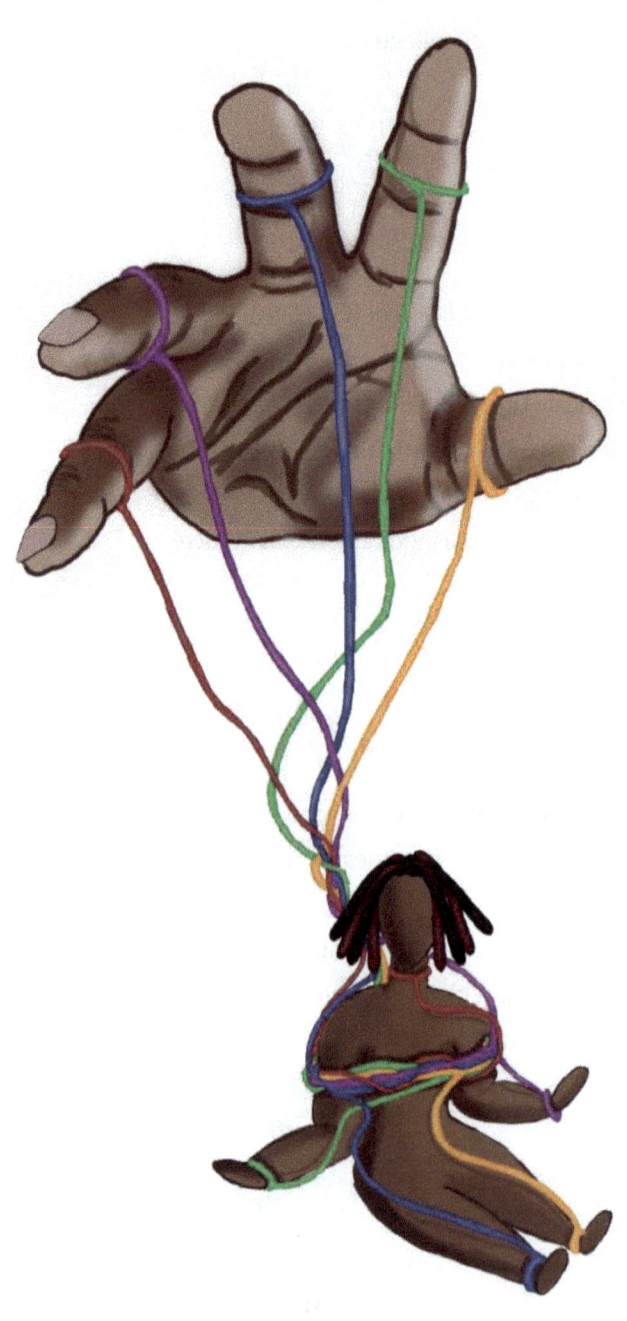

MARY'AH "MO'ZART" ONWUKWE

TWISTED STRINGS

You said, *"Let's just vibe, no strings attached."*
And I agreed as strings would only complicate things
but seeing the way your brown eyes lit up
when talking to me added a string.
You sending me funny pictures to cheer me up
when I felt down added a string.
The one too many nights we stayed up laughing,
enjoying each other's company added a string.
We consummated our union without a marriage
which added more strings than I could count.

A couple years down the line you ask me,
"Still no strings attached, right?"
And I nervously laugh, *"Yea, yea, no strings attached."*
while my whole body has been wrapped with strings
that are too dense to cut and instead
squeeze my flesh and slice me open
as I attempt to break free.
Pain oozes out of me with high viscosity.
Slow and tender.
Will this connection be the end of me?
Because you don't want me.
You want to remain with "no strings attached"
yet I am fully attached to you, and you don't care.
Or maybe you do,
and you're taking full advantage of my strings
that have twisted together and have been tied to your fingers

so that you could control me the way you wanted to.
I wasn't like putty in your hands,
but more like a ventriloquist dummy to your stage acts
with no applause at the end for your performance.

I always found it hard to say "*no*" to you.
I always found myself dropping everything to come rescue you.
If you told me to jump, I'd ask "how high?"
If you told me to walk a mile in your shoes,
I'd already be tying my shoelaces.
If you asked me to die for you,
I'd ask, "when would be most convenient?"
Your love was sick, twisted even,
just like these strings that I can't break free from.
I wish I could take scissors and cut them
but you won't orchestrate my hands to reach high enough.
I've tried leaving you and moving on with someone else
but whenever I get too far out of your grasp,
you tug me back to you, pulling me closer,
even though you know you don't want me.
You just don't want anyone else to have me
or lose your precious hold on me.

All these twisted strings connecting me to you forms a prison
I can't escape, a prison I can't even begin to unravel.
It has bunched together in a way that makes it difficult
to determine where one part ends and another begins.
I need help breaking free from these twisted strings.

MARY'AH "MO'ZART" ONWUKWE

Can anyone help me?

I'm falling into these bad habits which are twisting these strings
tighter around me because all they do is make me think of you.
I've tried to drink my pain away, it didn't help,
it only brought more of my pain to the surface.
I've tried to eat my pain away
and all I did was get fatter with grief
because these strings won't let go of me.
I've tried to laugh away the pain,
thinking that maybe if I smiled hard enough,
it would become genuine,
but instead, my smiles turned into grimaces,
as these strings twisted around me more, squeezing me tighter
making me fall deeper into this entanglement with you.

I've tried everything I could think of to sever this bond
but something won't allow it to break.
Sometimes I think maybe I'd be better off if I were dead.
Sometimes I question if death is the only way
these bonds would break
and if it's worth it, just to be free from you.
Because I can't have you in the way that I want you
and life just doesn't seem to be worth living anymore,
but it would be useless to try since our souls
tying together created a bond stronger than life,
stronger than death itself.
I don't think I'll ever break free from you.

DAYDREAMS & NIGHTMAREZ

Even when my twisted strings are attached to you,
you are not bonded to me.
You never were,
even though you pretended to be
because you said "no strings attached"
and you meant it.
I thought I did too.

MARY'AH "MO'ZART" ONWUKWE

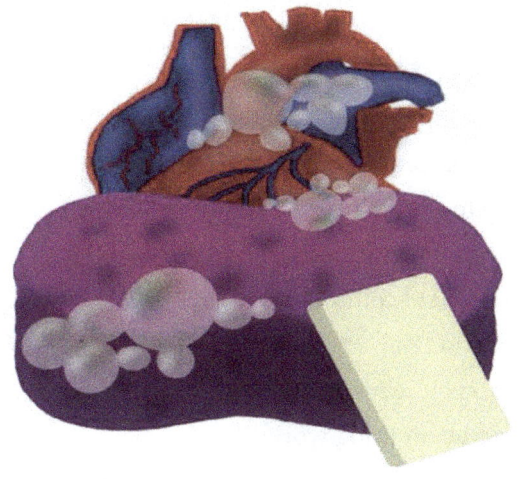

RESIDUE

They say dreams are instances of other lifetimes,
so, does that mean in every lifetime we are doomed to fail?
Because ever since we separated,
the moment you are in my dreams,
my eyes water with sadness,
and I wake up drowning in a sea of sorrow
that I didn't even realize was that deep.
I thought I got over you,
but it appears that it was only surface level.

No matter how many times
I've washed you from my brain
and washed away all the harsh and hurt feelings I felt about you,
pieces of you and those feelings
still remain like residue.

DAYDREAMS & NIGHTMAREZ

Staining me permanently.
Haunting me fervently.
I can't escape you.
Was the pain you caused not enough
that you have to keep resurfacing
to remind me at the worst times?
I tried to be all that I could be for you
and it wasn't enough.
What more do you want from me?
I scrub and scrub, nothing works.
You're more stubborn than the dish from mom's spaghetti.
I know it's clean, just stained.
Just like I know I should be clean with all this washing
but I can't help but feel dirty
with the parts of you that still stick to me.

Scrub… scrub
I hate your beautiful smile.
Scrub…scrub
Why did you have to make me laugh so much?
Scrub…scrub
Your harmonious voice singing melodies
echoes in my head, why won't it shut up!
Scrub…scrub
Your hugs and kisses feel engraved into my skin,
gotta get them off!
Scrub… scrub
Your fingerprints won't fade away no matter how hard I

MARY'AH "MO'ZART" ONWUKWE

Scrub...scrub

I miss my bestfriend that I could go and talk to about any and everything.

Who am I supposed to go to now?

Scrub...scrub

Why didn't you want me?

Why didn't you choose me?

Scrub...scrub

What did those other girls have that I didn't?

Scrub...scrub

I can't believe I wasted 4 years of my life begging to be yours.

How could I have been so stupid?

Scrub...scrub

Why do I still love you despite everything?

Scrub...scrub

You left me long ago.

Scrub...scrub

So why won't your residue come off?

DAYDREAMS & NIGHTMAREZ

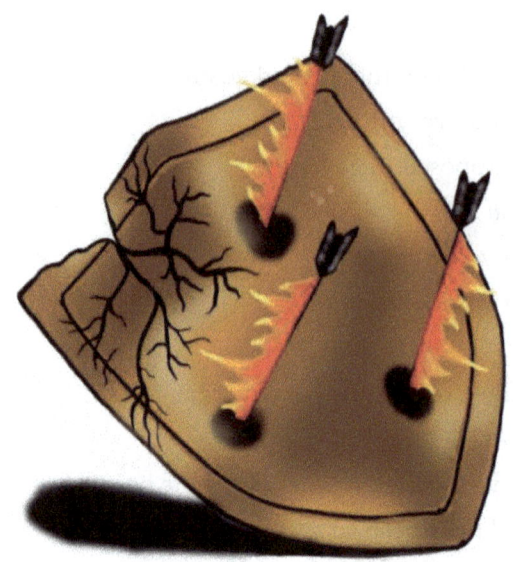

FALLEN SOLDIER

They say that God gives His toughest battles
to His strongest soldiers.
Well maybe God made a mistake,
because I'm not strong enough to carry this weight,
this burden that has been placed on me.
I'm on this battlefield fighting for the Lord
and I feel like I'm fighting alone,
deserted and helpless. I know God is there,
but it doesn't feel like it.
The mind and heart are separate entities,
so, what I think and what I feel may not always align.
I know that He's watching over me. I know that He cares.
But this enemy is so strong. It just makes me feel
like He's never there because this weight feels too heavy to bear.

MARY'AH "MO'ZART" ONWUKWE

I need a break from this madness. Why is this happening to me?
I used to be much better than this, but the enemy doesn't care.
He just keeps deploying his tricks to hurt me
in the worst ways by using his snares and it's working.
And because I keep falling into temptation.
I have become a fallen soldier
on a battlefield I didn't create.
I'm fighting for my Savior, yet I just feel like bait,
like I am being used to lure the enemy into a trap,
yet I am the one who becomes enslaved,
enslaved to thoughts like I have to fight this battle on my own,
and that I'm not good enough to be chosen for a higher purpose.
I've put on the armor of God,
but I feel like it's defective
because it's not protecting me from each blow
that the enemy uses to strike me.

My belt of Truth had been cut down from my waistline,
so, my sword of the Spirit is lost on the battlefield with it,
now I have trouble keeping up with God's Truth
and the enemy's lies.
Both pieces of armor lie somewhere covered with the guilt
of not spending time in my Word like I did with everything else
so, I've been forced to fight hand to hand with the enemy.
It's so hard to fight physically with something I can't see.
My breastplate of righteousness had been penetrated
with spears and swords of the enemy.
Sin slithered through the cracks in my armor

and I found myself poisoned with venom,
becoming infected with its nature.
My shield of faith had been heavily fractured
and is punctured from the flaming arrows
the enemy has thrown at me.
Doubt creeped its way into my head
that maybe God has abandoned me,
and won't come to help me with this fight.
My helmet of Salvation hadn't been tugged on so tight
because I started to question
if Christ could truly die for such a sinner as I,
just one of many thoughts the enemy has planted in my head.
My feet, prepared with shoes of the Gospel of Peace,
had been loosened while I wasn't looking. And I tripped
into worrying about my future and my fate
at the end of this battle. I didn't stand a chance.

I've tried to weather through every attack,
but the constant rain caused my armor to rust and crack.
I have an enemy fighting me on every side,
I can't defend myself. It's matching me stride for stride
so yea I can put my pride aside
and say that I'm not strong enough to battle this enemy alone.
He whispers in my ear that I'm not good enough, that I'll die
here, and that I don't deserve to keep fighting.
His words cut like daggers, piercing me
through this broken armor that has me now lying

on the ground and I'm starting to think that I won't make it out.
This must be the end for me.
I am dying on the battlefield. Waiting,
waiting for my imminent demise
because this enemy of mine is so wise.
It snakes its way into my head and places its poison in my brain.
My throat and lungs swell and tighten
as I call out to my fellow comrades
but no one can hear me, so no one can help me. I'm all alone.
No one knows what I'm going through. No one's felt what I felt.
No one can understand. I can't break free. I can't go on.
I'm losing this fight.
This great big enemy relishes every tear that falls from my eyes.
It's so hard to stay strong when all I wanna be is weak. I'm tired
of having to put up a facade when everything is going wrong.

Can't God see I'm not strong enough?
I've been battered, blemished, and broken.
I'm lying on the battlefield bleeding,
my wounds oozing the pain I couldn't share.
My wounds, widening beyond repair. I need a doctor.
I'm on the battlefield fighting to stay alive. It's no easy feat.
My adversary keeps urging me to give up and give in.
I lie on the ground accepting my fate, that this battle I can't win.
This death doesn't come with honor but shame and guilt,
because I wasn't strong enough
to beat this enemy on my battlefield.
I fought the good fight and maybe I should give up.

DAYDREAMS & NIGHTMAREZ

Or maybe I'll be slain and finally receive relief
because I won't have to suffer anymore.
I won't have to fight anymore.
Maybe I'll be recognized for how good of a fight I put up.
But it doesn't matter, because regardless of how I'm viewed,
I'll still remain a fallen soldier.

SUNSET

DAYDREAMS & NIGHTMAREZ

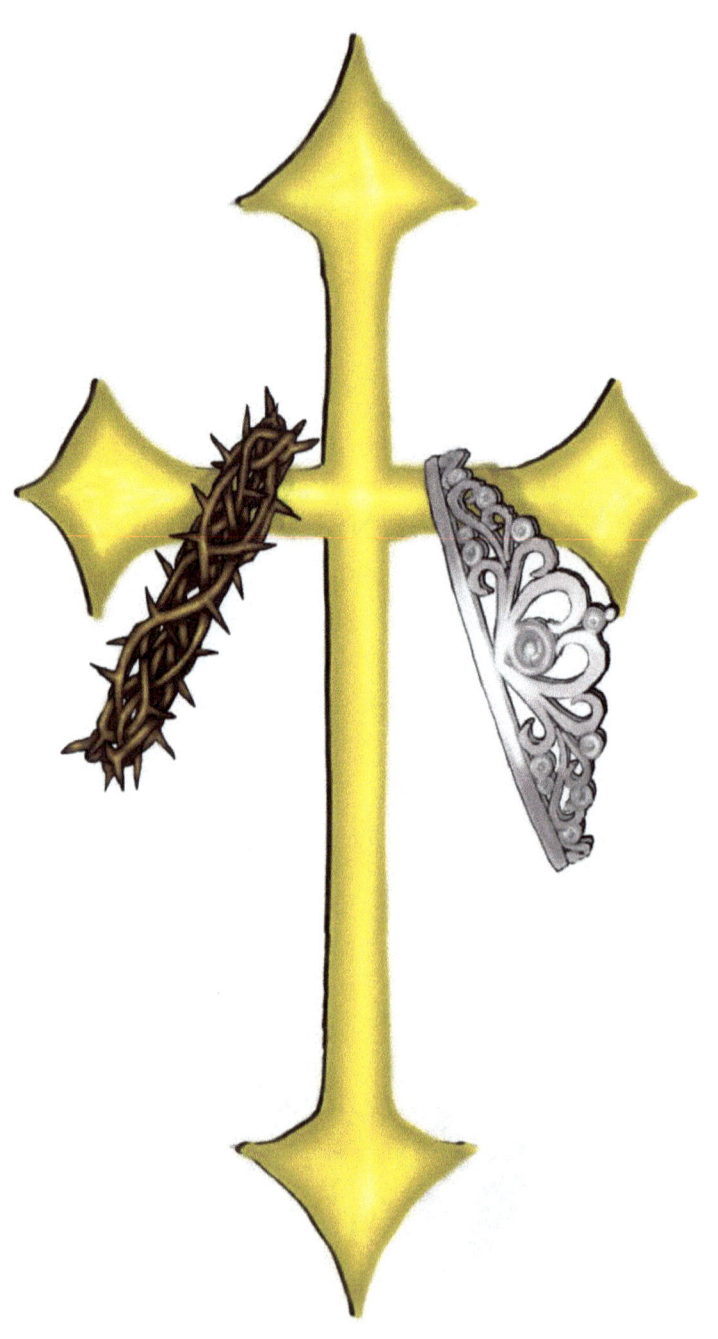

MARY'AH "MO'ZART" ONWUKWE

POWER COUPLE

The next relationship I'm in will be a powerful one.
We will be a power couple,
not just because we are building empires,
but because of the power that we have instilled in us
to cast out devils in high places.
Power so great that it makes Hell afraid
because we leave no stone unturned.
The armor of our union suits us in battle. We stand firm,
ready for the enemy's next attack
as our belts of truth are strapped to our waist
holding our weapons of mass destruction. Our swords
of the Spirit reflect our light and slash through
the lies of the enemy with God's Truth.
Our breastplates of righteousness have been divinely cultivated
with the most durable metals to protect us from the temptations
of sin. Our shields of faith deflect and extinguish
the flaming arrows of confusion and doubt from the evil one.
Our helmets of salvation are secured tightly onto our heads
to protect us from the deceitfulness of the enemy to plant dark
thoughts in our minds. Our feet, prepared with the Gospel
of Peace, allow us to move confidently
forward in rough terrain to share the goodness of Our Father
with lost souls on the battlefield.

We will strengthen the core of our relationship
as we pray together and for each other
while we meditate on Our Father's Word, day and night.

DAYDREAMS & NIGHTMAREZ

The love we share will remain immortal,
forever fresh and young.
We've both been heavily anointed
to carry out missions for Our Father.
We are filled with a light that drives out any darkness
to help free those trapped inside it.
I'll lead the souls out as He'll save and redeem them.
We will spread our gifts from the Spirit
and live in our purpose imitating and glorifying Our Father.
The enemy may try to come against our union
to disrupt our progress but no weapons, or people,
formed against us shall prosper.
The evil one rages at how we are still alive and still standing,
surviving every snare meant to entrap us.
We together have defeated death, so it has lost its sting.
I will be able to walk through the valley of the shadow of death
and not fear any evil cuz I got God and You by my side.
When I stumble, He will uplift me where I am weak.
He doesn't hold my past failures against me.
He encourages me to get back up and keep fighting
alongside Him. He reminds me that He will always be
by my side and will never forsake me.
He knows that I am not perfect, and He loves me anyway,
despite my imperfections.

In my next relationship, we will be a force to be reckoned with,
Jesus and I joined together in holy matrimony,
the perfect power couple.

MARY'AH "MO'ZART" ONWUKWE

THE EYE OF THE STORM

A sudden, raging storm startles me.
Just when I think to move to find shelter,
the Lord commands me, *"Peace, be still and know that I am God."*
I follow His command as He reminds me
that being in the eye of the storm is the safest place I can be.
The one place the storm can't touch.
I am anointed and protected
so, God shields me from the enemy's attacks on my mind.
The enemy cannot touch me
so, he's forced to shake up the environment surrounding me
by uprooting my finances, so that it withers and dies
while my bills continue to soar to the sky;
by crushing my physical health
with the heavy wreckage of my temple;
by swirling my failures around me,

trying to eradicate the peace I have within;
and by crumbling the relationship I had
with a guy I thought I'd spend forever with.
The efforts of the enemy are futile
because even though the ground around me
falls away like sinking sand, I stand on a solid rock
that has laid a stable foundation that will not waver
against the disastrous storm around me.
I hadn't always known but I function best
when chaos surrounds me.
God has trusted me with this storm.
He knows that I will grow through it
and come out stronger than before.
He knows that my lips will still bless His name
despite the storm.
My praises will still be sung with a joyful noise
and my heart will be ever more filled with thanksgiving.

If you are experiencing a storm and you are troubled by it,
ask yourself if you are in the eye of the storm.
If you are not, stop moving to try and fight it and be still,
because otherwise you'll only feel the brunt of the storm more.
While in the eye of the storm,
you will find that God's peace and warmth will surround you
and shelter you in His strong tower against the enemy.
You will remain grounded
as long as you keep your eyes lifted to the Hills
because your help will come from the Lord.

MARY'AH "MO'ZART" ONWUKWE

Before you ask why you are even experiencing a storm, please
understand that just because God is with you,
it doesn't mean that you won't experience any storms,
it just means that you will have peace through them.
In the meantime, look at what is being disrupted around you
and change your perspective.
Please consider that maybe God allowed the storm
to destroy these things before they destroyed you.
Maybe there is a lesson you needed to grasp
and the storm is the only way
that God could grab your attention to learn it.
Please remember to praise your way through the storm
instead of complaining.
Gratitude changes attitude.
The enemy will become more furious
that you decide to bless your Creator despite its best efforts.
It may cause the storm to rage more,
but after you have suffered for a while,
He will make you perfect, and establish, strengthen,
and settle you. The storm will begin to cease
as it will no longer have any more of your pain fueling it.
The enemy will realize that he cannot affect you
and will be defeated
as you stay immersed in total peace.

DAYDREAMS & NIGHTMAREZ

GOD'S HAND

Some days I sit back and think about God's Hand in my life.
He's been such a strong tower against the enemy
and its weak attempt to cause me strife.
God holds the whole world in His Hand,
so why should I worry about what tomorrow holds
and demands when I could appreciate the life that I have today?
It's okay for me to ask God for assistance,
but I will not be troubled by the troubles of this world,
no matter how much they are persistent.
God will supply where I am lacking
and He will strengthen me where I feel like cracking.
God's Hand is everywhere in my life.

People often have trouble accepting God's divine plan,
not knowing that He has a purpose for everything in His Hand.

MARY'AH "MO'ZART" ONWUKWE

Just as characters and obstacles are put in the story for the
author's purpose, God places people and struggles into my life
for His purpose to serve me. He has full control over my life,
and I have free will. Or so I think,
because there are times where I think I am choosing
for myself but it had already been predestined for me
to make certain mistakes so that I could learn by experience,
where just words alone couldn't teach me.

I learned almost the hard way not to drink and drive.
Let me explain what I mean and why I'm blessed to be alive.
Picture this: You're having fun with your sis,
and she offers you a drink. It was about a 4-ounce mixture of
Hennessy and fruit punch. You take a moment to think,
Why not? You know you're a lightweight,
but you could use this to hydrate. It can't affect me that much.
Taking the first sip, it immediately hits your senses in a rush
and you feel it tingling in your head. Despite this,
you drink the rest of it and the sensations spread.
It's time to leave for an open mic night and you decide to drive
thinking that you are sober enough to safely arrive.
As you put on your shoes, you placed them on the wrong feet
and laughed it off thinking that you are so silly.
Standing up, you stumble, and for a second, start to see double
but shake it off to try and get it out of your system.
With wisdom, you instruct your two passengers
to put on their fasteners before you started on your way.
You pray over the car that God will guide you today

safely to your destination. Seconds after praying
you are riding down the street, surveying,
and notice cars riding through the intersection adjacent to you.
You become filled with rage that the cars were going through
and being rude to you for doing so when not told.
So, you step on the gas and speed down the road.
Just as you approach the intersection, you notice the light is red.
But by now, you're already under it, so you go ahead.
A truck that was meant to T-bone you on your side,
stops, as if it was denied
as you speed right out of the intersection.
And just after passing it, you snap out of it and question
what happened and what almost happened.
Immediately you fill with guilt and apologize repeatedly
to your passengers for putting their lives in danger stupidly.
At the open mic night, you can't even enjoy yourself
because you feel so convicted for endangering your health.
You then hear a voice speak loud and explicit to your spirit,
"Let this be the first and the last time you try something like this.
I will not save you the next time." You listen and don't resist.
You realize that God's Hand blocked that car from hitting yours
and thank God for keeping you and your friends uninjured.

Trusting God is not easy at times.
He can keep us waiting for certain promises and signs
because we aren't ready. Or simply because instead, He
wants to see if we have enough faith to know that He is God
whether we received our promise or not.

MARY'AH "MO'ZART" ONWUKWE

He wants us to be able to know without a shadow of doubt
that everything is adorning a spot in His Hand.
A perfect illustration of trusting God
occurred on a random Sunday morning.
Imagine waking up early, and you and your brother get dressed
for church. Heading outside to your car, you assessed
that the air was humid as the skies were gray.
A fresh layer of rain glistened on the roads
as you went on your way.
The roads were clear. As you traveled on 695 for a while,
you noticed a car crashed into a guardrail on a random mile
with smoke coming from it and its owner standing beside it.
You pray that God will help them and permit them to stay safe.
A minute or two afterwards, a sweet smell starts to disrupt
your ride. It smelt like maple syrup.
You passed it off as being the surrounding area's odor.
Soon, your car decelerated on its own as you pressed the motor.
Confused, you pulled your car easily over to the shoulder
as no other cars were around. Moments later, the hood smoked
as the check engine light came on. A cry, these events invoked
because you didn't know what was wrong with your car.
You dialed your mother to ask for help as this was bizarre.
She called a tow company and told you not to worry,
that everything would be alright she guarantees.
You texted a group chat with your cousins and had a discussion
about how scared and upset you were since it hadn't been a year
of you driving your car yet, only a few months
and you needed it for school. Your cousin tells you once,

DAYDREAMS & NIGHTMAREZ

"Let go and let God." You don't understand what she meant
until in your head, a thought presents:
your car broke down while the highway was empty.
If it had decelerated the way it did with plenty cars around,
you could've gotten into a bad accident or been in the ground.
Then you realized that God's Hand broke down your vehicle
while no one could hurt you or your brother, it was strategical.

God's Hand has surrounded me and protected me from harm,
but has also pushed me into opportunities
that I couldn't have received on my own.
It's incredible to think that such a magnificent God
could care so much
about little ole me. I am a speck amongst the millions
of other people, yet He chose me to be His.
He purchased me and now watches over me
because of my worth to Him.
I am priceless but God also knows that I am not perfect
and will put myself in harm's way without trying,
that is why He protects me from unforeseen dangers.
He knows the purpose that He has for me,
and I have yet to complete it,
so, He uses His Hand to guide me to safety.

As you have read, I am a visual type of girl,
so let me paint a good example that will give you a whirl.
You are new to the city and decide to take the bus
for the first time by yourself to adjust to the city life.

MARY'AH "MO'ZART" ONWUKWE

You used your phone as a guide to your grandmother's
from your college, UMBC. You and others
are just finishing freshman orientation
so, you have quite a few bags with you. Misreading information
leads you onto the wrong bus because it's the first one
that showed up in a while and you wanted to get out of the sun.
This bus was still heading in the same direction, so, you stayed.
You get off the first bus to catch the second and were dismayed
because you have no clue where the next stop is. A beep
from the bus driver steers you in the right direction. You peep
the stop and attempt to cross the street in a hurry. Not heeding
the turning cars before proceeding, you hit a wall you can't see
as the car turning the corner seemed unaware of your body.
After it completes its turn, you notice your next bus arriving
at your stop. You don't think much about surviving
as you rush across the street once more.
Lugging your bags, you hit an invisible wall like before
but more harshly as a car zooms past you
centimeters from where you stood as if you were see-through,
as if it sped up to hit you. One more inch forward
and your body would've been disordered
on impact. You don't have time to think
as it happened in a blink, so you rush onto the bus
and pay your fare. Taking a seat and a few seconds to adjust,
you think about what transpired:
you were almost hit by a car twice more than desired;
you also hit an invisible wall twice.
Thinking about the walls you hit, they were precise,

and you realize they weren't walls at all,
but God's Hand that caused your movements to halt.
Through the experience, you started to thank God
for being your wall.

God has saved me on numerous accounts,
not only my physical body but my soul as well.
Through His Son shedding His blood and losing His life,
I can live eternally with Our Father in Heaven and not hell.
He gave me the gift of salvation
that never expires and is mine.
A gift that could never be plucked from God's divine Hand.
He has chosen me, and I am His.
Because of God's Hand, I can walk into the purpose
that He has given me and conquer my fears.
Because of God's Hand, I found my ability to speak
in a creative tongue that allows me to express myself in ways
that I never thought to be possible.
Because of God's Hand, you are reading my words
at just the moment you were meant to.

MARY'AH "MO'ZART" ONWUKWE

HEALING WOUNDS

I lost you.

And you.

And you.

And you.

The amalgamation of all these losses grew

as they created so many open wounds all over my body.

Wounds that required stitches--sloppy,

had been covered with Band-Aids

and now I need some advanced aids

because they still sting and now are infected.

They didn't go undetected

as they leaked into my everyday routine.

DAYDREAMS & NIGHTMAREZ

Infections so obscene, I landed right into a hospital for healing.
Now I'm dealing with those surrounding me.
Of course, I see sick people.
But some were pretending, so they could take advantage
of my weakness. They were really sick people and evil.
They scoured the hospital to search for the scent of infection.
They say it smells sweet as the projection of the scents:
resentment, worthlessness and low self-esteem
made me an easy target to prey upon as they scheme.
They dangled a way to heal me in my face
knowing I'll chase them without hesitation
until it was too late to realize their violation.
Feeling too burnt out, I refused to have any participation
in healing myself.

Unbeknownst to me, as they left with the pieces they've stolen,
some of the infection sites advanced so bad — swollen,
so, now they are necrotic. My life is now chaotic
due to the parts of me that are dying
because I refused to heal.
My doctor tells me that He must deal with these infected parts
before He can treat the necrotic tissue
because with this issue still spreading inside me,
it will just cause more of my flesh to die.
He finds where this infection originated, and I cry.
It's been so long since I've acknowledged my wounds
and the pain I once tuned out, has ballooned.
My doctor handles me with care as He treats me

MARY'AH "MO'ZART" ONWUKWE

with His Love that comes from the Heavens above,
so that I can be free. He replenishes my body
with His son's blood that was shed
so that I wouldn't be dying anymore, but instead,
have everlasting life. In doing so, every other wound that stems
from this wound can be cleansed as well.

Moving onto treat the necrotic tissue fast,
my doctor tells me that it cannot be saved and must be cast
and amputated for me to survive.
He lets me know that if I wait too long,
there will be nothing left to revive.
I would just be a hollow shell with a dying spirit.
He asks me, am I ready to let go of these dead parts of me so that
I can move on?
I hesitate to respond.

He reassures me that cutting off this necrotic flesh
can leave room for reinvention to progress.
He tells me to take solace in knowing that I can cultivate
and activate new characteristics that can offset the old.
I can unfold as a totally different person
than I was when I arrived. With some assertion,
I could become an entirely new being that can start again
from experience instead of from scratch.
He tells me that it can be intense
but that He will not forsake me as I learn these new parts
of me and restart my journey.

DAYDREAMS & NIGHTMAREZ

He affirms that He'll be there to help every step of the way.
He asks today, do I trust Him?
and offers His Hand.

I take it. The doctor smiles and continues with His plan
to cut off the dead flesh. He informs me that wounds
often allude to disobedience
and advises that I should stay away from the activities
that created these wounds. And instead, lower the susceptibility
of creating them by using the wounds as a reminder
of what I survived and healed from
to be wiser in my next choices.

He instructs me that if I ever find myself lost again,
that He always recommends me to return free of charge
to find healing and a new direction.

He mentions that healing my wounds aren't
just a one-stop-then-done correction,
it will continue for the rest of my days.
He reassures me to not be dismayed
as He has contacted my family and friends and teachers
who can make features in my life and guide me
through these new stages of growth that I will enter.
They can softly speak love into me—tender,
so that I can embrace these new parts of me.
He informs me there will be situations, and sometimes people,
which can trigger the reopening of the healed wounds

MARY'AH "MO'ZART" ONWUKWE

that I may think are lethal but are only exposed
so that new areas of myself can start to heal. He discloses
that it is normal and a sign that I am growing as a person.
Each stage of elevation requires separation
from the parts of me that could cause myself to worsen and
will no longer serve me in the next step in my journey.
This should not deter me, but I should accept
that it is all for my good and that sometimes,
change is necessary for growth.
The last thing He tells me as a close and to conclude
is that as long as I have wounds,
I need to heal, and that I shouldn't feel afraid to start.

DAYDREAMS & NIGHTMAREZ

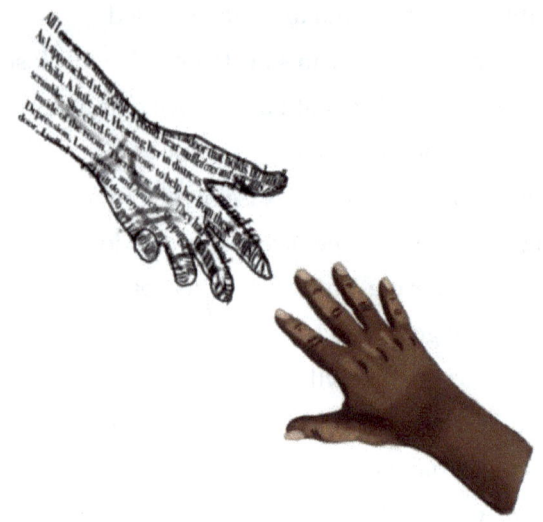

POETRY SAVED ME

All I can see is a room with a sleek metal door that holds no handle. As I approached the door, I could hear muffled cries and screams of a child. A little girl. Hearing her in distress caused my mind to scramble. She cried for someone to help her from these monsters inside of the room. There were three. They had been named Depression, Loneliness, and Anxiety.

Slapping my hand on the door, I yelled out, "I will do everything in my power to help you. I'm coming to get you to safety."

Pushing the door, it wouldn't nudge. Taking a few paces back, I charged at the door, it wouldn't budge. I tried everything I could think of, but to no avail. I leaned against the door and slid to the floor feeling defeated and ever so frail. With my head between my knees, I sobbed. God, watching from above, heard my cries, and decided to give me a helping hand to show His Love. He sent a man into my life who noticed my helplessness. I rambled on to him about my situation of trying to save the little girl with an emphasis. The man listened with intent. He told me that he couldn't open the door for me, but that he had a solution, so without another word, he went.

When he returned, he had a lady beside him and introduced me to his friend. Her name was Poetry and when she saw me, her knees took a bend as the man left us with some business to attend. She saw my red eyes and tear-stained face and wrapped me in her warm embrace. "What's wrong?" She softly asked.

"There's a little girl inside the room who needs me and this door I can't get past." She nodded her head once and sat down beside me. Her perfume filled my nostrils and calmed me for she smelt like a mixture of lavender and sweet pea. I explained to her that I know about the monsters the little girl is facing. They had tormented me almost my whole life and were enslaving.

Depression, as I called its name, it reared its ugly head. It was a large black beast that casted a cold, heavy shadow wherever it had tread. The beast had dozens of eyes that held me under scrutiny that made me feel like I could do nothing right. It oozed pain and sorrow all day and night. As it growled at me, its breath suffocated me of my worth and happiness. No matter how much I tried to escape, it found me and punished me for my attempted craftiness. Each tear that dropped from my eye, the creature licked up with its slippery tongue. Feeling its poisonous saliva on my face and covering my wounds always stung. It fueled the wicked beast, and I shivered in fear. Poetry remained unafraid as she grabbed my hand to remind me that she was near.

She commanded the beast to back away and it listened. She stood and pulled me up to stand with her, and I stiffened. "How did you command the beast so effortlessly?" I asked incredulously.

She told me, "This beast cannot hold any power over you unless you allow it. You can choose to not believe the lies it tells you. You *are* loved. You *are* enough. You *are* beautiful, *just the way you are*." My eyes welled with tears as Poetry told me exactly what I had been longing to hear. She pointed at the beast and continued to say, "Now, you need to look Depression in its eyes and tell it that its reign ends today."

Staring into its dozens of eyes, I questioned if I could actually defeat the ugly beast named Depression. Poetry grabbed my hand and she looked at me with a determined expression. I inhaled the strength that she possessed.

I nodded my head and turned to the beast and confessed, "You may have had your fun stealing my joy, but you will steal it from me no more. I demand my happiness back. I command that you depart so that I can get my life on track. I declare you defeated in the name of Jesus, and I, victorious."

The beast glared at me yet heeded my words and the sight of him leaving was glorious.

I jumped for joy when Poetry stopped me and said, "We have defeated one monster, yet two still remain. We can't rejoice too much just yet, until the other two are slain. Call on the next monster."

I nodded my head and did as she said. As I called on the next monster, Loneliness, it appeared. Every time it came around, everyone and everything surrounding me cleared. Poetry disappeared and I stood alone. This particular monster relished in the fact that its physical identity remained unknown. For it was invisible. But that didn't mean it lacked in ways of making me feel miserable. It weighs you down with chains of self-doubt, lethargy, and worthlessness. Chains that felt like they would never break as if they were made with permanence. Loneliness made my heart ache for the closeness of friends and family, but there was never anyone in my reach. I could screech to the hilltops for companions yet I'm the person everyone abandons. Not even Poetry wanted to stick around. Then a thought struck me that was so profound. I am never good enough to make people stay. Maybe that's why it is so easy for them to walk away.

A lone tear escaped my eye as I looked to the sky. "Lord, why did you abandon me when I needed you most?"

I felt big arms engulf me with comfort as I became filled with the Holy Ghost. The chains lifted as I started to feel as light as a feather. My vision cleared revealing the room again along with Poetry, like a cloud revealing the sun after stormy weather.

Next, Poetry started to quote, "God will never leave nor forsake you. He's always there watching over you when you are not aware. So, you will never be alone with Him by your side."

My eyes opened wide, "God came to visit little ole me and wrapped me in his arms of love?"

Poetry smiled and said, "Yes, because you are one of His children that He loves and cares for from up above. You are special to God and not just another number. He knows you by name and knows just what you need before you can even wonder. All we have to do is call on Him and He is present. He's there when you are happy and even closer when we feel unpleasant. When two or three are gathered together in His name, He's in the midst. God saw that you needed a friend, so He brought me to you to assist."

I squeezed Poetry tight as I knew Loneliness lost this fight.

I spoke again, "I think I'm ready for the last creature." Poetry nodded her head to let me know that she was ready for it to make its feature.

I called Anxiety, the last of the creatures, and it appeared filling me with dread. My heart raced tenfold as so many horrible thoughts rushed to my head that centered around the little girl and the possibility of her being dead. Tears fell like an avalanche down my face, starting with one then multiplying by a ton. My lungs had trouble capturing the air I needed to breathe. The walls were caving in beneath my feet. The crippling feeling caused me great unease. Anxiety wore a smug as it watched me fall to my knees.

Poetry grabs my forearms and says, "Tell me your fears."

"You can't help her. She's too far gone." The creature said with a yawn.

Poetry continued unfazed by the interruption, "This creature thrives off confusion and corruption. Unless you voice your fears, you cannot overcome them. Because what you do not acknowledge, stays hidden and becomes a blockage to your buried potential."

I sighed before I replied, "I'm scared that I can't save the little girl. That I'll be too late to rescue her from an untimely fate."

Poetry smiled and said, "Okay, good. Now tell me what you hear."

Opening my ears, I listened. The little girl was cheering me on from inside the room and my eyes glistened. I smiled, stood, and turned toward Anxiety. "You took my fears and turned them against me. But it's too bad for you that I have a remedy to the uncertainty. I know that I can walk through the valley of the shadow of death and fear no evil, because I now know that God is with me. I also know that no weapon formed against me shall prosper. So, I banish you from my life." I spoke firmly as I straightened my posture.

The creature let out a gut-wrenching scream before he disappeared because I foiled his scheme.

Poetry cheesed before she expressed, "We have defeated all monsters and laid them to rest. Now let's open this door and leave the little girl waiting no more."

We turned towards the room and once again faced the sleek metal door. There was now a handle, so I turned it and I froze when I saw her, my jaw dropping to the floor.

For the little girl, was a younger version of me.

This little girl is now free.

She can now jump around and play with the other warm fuzzy feelings that had been previously locked and stored away. She had been so scared of the monsters that hid in my closet and underneath my bed that she became paralyzed in the bedroom of my mind, unable to move because she didn't want to die. The beasts prevented me from loving, caring for, and protecting her, so, she sports a few scars from their attacks. With each beast defeated for now, her and I both could relax. Looking at her, I realized that I am now the person my inner child can run to for safety. I made a promise to myself to protect her from harm and care for her faithfully.

I reached out my arms and she ran into them as I hugged her so tight for all that she's endured throughout her existence.

She breathed a sigh of relief and thanked me for my persistence.

I ran my fingers through her kinky hair and told her that you are enough,

I love you,

and for her, I'll always be there.

It brought tears to my eyes that filled with glee. I also told her that she is now my number one priority.

MARY'AH "MO'ZART" ONWUKWE

She gazes up at me and smiles with loving eyes. I returned it as I felt the warmth of her smile along with a few butterflies.

With the little girl still in my arms, I glanced over at Poetry and thanked her for saving me.

**THANK YOU FOR READING.
I HOPE YOU ENJOYED THE JOURNEY.
COME BACK TO VISIT ANYTIME.**

MARY'AH "MO'ZART" ONWUKWE

ABOUT THE AUTHOR

Mary'ah Onwukwe, also known as "Mo'zArt" when performing, is a poet, African-American fiction writer, artist, and now published author. She's created a business called Mo'zArt Creationz to reflect her talents and gifts and share them with the world. She's been a true creative at heart since she could learn to write and read.

She always had a love for poetry but didn't know she had the ability to write it until January of 2022. Ever since then, she's grown and began healing herself through writing about her emotions and traumas in a creative format. Just as she started the process to heal herself, she wanted to be of help to others by helping them to heal. She believes that this is her purpose in life, whether she does it through her actions or her words.

ABOUT MO'ZART CREATIONZ

Mo'zArt Creationz, LLC is a business that was created to be able to glorify God through sharing my gifts with others. I make commissioned portraits and offer graphic design services. Each piece I make is an original, so take joy in having a one-of-a-kind portrait or graphic! If that isn't enough, I also write poetry, novels, and journals. So, if portraits aren't your cup of tea, then dive into my mind as you journal about your life and read about some of my innermost thoughts and my wildest daydreams come to life!

If you like any of my graphics included in this poetry book and would like a canvas, poster, t-shirt, or any other merchandise item of it, feel free to contact me through my website, www.mozartcreationz.com.

www.ingramcontent.com/pod-product-compliance
Lightning Source LLC
Chambersburg PA
CBHW072045160426
43197CB00014B/2634